"Warmly relatable and incredibly p_____ _____ small _____ great things, or, better said, makes it possible for readers to achieve great things. He presents more than anyone could ever accomplish before tenure (or maybe in a lifetime of teaching), but that means this will be a volume educators will want to keep readily accessible. I know this will benefit my students who are training for the academy because it has already been a tangible benefit to me."

Amy Peeler, associate professor of New Testament at Wheaton College and Graduate School

"Mike Kibbe has a rare gift for being able to pass along not just the content of his expertise but the process that got him there. He shares his hard-earned wisdom for teaching well without losing your soul in the process. The result is a lively and engaging tutorial in the art of becoming a world-class professor. I couldn't put it down. Grab a copy for every recent PhD you know in Bible, theology, or related disciplines. They'll thank you!"

Carmen Joy Imes, associate professor of Old Testament at Prairie College in Three Hills, Alberta, and author of *Bearing God's Name: Why Sinai Still Matters*

"The outline set forth in Kibbe's book facilitates a paradigm shift for graduate students, is career-altering for professors, and is valuable for administrators who desire to partner with impactful educators. This is a master guide from a skilled and experienced practitioner who is deeply concerned about his students' educational experience as well as contributing to the academic community. What an invaluable read for all who are interested in experiencing the redoubled advantages of advanced study within the learning environment—from those ambitious scholars who want to teach well to passionate teachers who wish to incorporate advanced scholarship into their instruction!"

Dominick S. Hernández, assistant professor of Old Testament interpretation, director del Programa Hispano en Línea, The Southern Baptist Theological Seminary

"If only I could go back in time and give this book to my former self! To be honest, though, Michael Kibbe's *From Research to Teaching* still taught the current me plenty. It not only gave this midcareer scholar some really handy teaching ideas, but more importantly, the Lord used it to renew my passion for the classroom, my commitment to excellence in every course, and my overall joy in doing what I do. As in life so also in print, Kibbe is brilliant, honest, humble, and fun, making this book extraordinarily insightful and thoroughly entertaining."

Joseph R. Dodson, associate professor of New Testament at Denver Seminary

FROM RESEARCH TO TEACHING

A GUIDE TO BEGINNING YOUR CLASSROOM CAREER

MICHAEL KIBBE

Foreword by Gary M. Burge

ivp
Academic
An imprint of InterVarsity Press
Downers Grove, Illinois

InterVarsity Press
P.O. Box 1400, Downers Grove, IL 60515-1426
ivpress.com
email@ivpress.com

InterVarsity Press® is the book-publishing division of InterVarsity Christian Fellowship/USA®, a movement of students and faculty active on campus at hundreds of universities, colleges, and schools of nursing in the United States of America, and a member movement of the International Fellowship of Evangelical Students. For information about local and regional activities, visit intervarsity.org.

Cover design and image composite: David Fassett
Interior design: Daniel van Loon
Images: blue ladder–stacked books: © jayk7 / Moment Collection / Getty Images
         podium: © inhauscreative / E+ / Getty Images

ISBN 978-0-8308-3918-6 (print)
ISBN 978-0-8308-3919-3 (digital)

Printed in the United States of America ♾

InterVarsity Press is committed to ecological stewardship and to the conservation of natural resources in all our operations. This book was printed using sustainably sourced paper.

Library of Congress Cataloging-in-Publication Data
A catalog record for this book is available from the Library of Congress.

| **P** | 25 | 24 | 23 | 22 | 21 | 20 | 19 | 18 | 17 | 16 | 15 | 14 | 13 | 12 | 11 | 10 | 9 | 8 | 7 | 6 | 5 | 4 | 3 | 2 | 1 |
| **Y** | 37 | 36 | 35 | 34 | 33 | 32 | 31 | 30 | 29 | 28 | 27 | 26 | 25 | 24 | 23 | 22 | 21 |

To Gary Burge,

who always made the best suggestions,

and Mark Jonas,

who always asked the hardest questions.

I am grateful to be counted among your pupils.

CONTENTS

FOREWORD

GARY M. BURGE

Some years back I was in the Navy. We completed a lot of training, learning how to escape a flooding ship, how to put out a fire, and even how to get out of a crashed and sinking helicopter that flipped upside down in fifty feet of water. In the helo, we learned how to use all of the onboard gear, from radio headsets to the five-point safety harness. I could even kick out a window safely if the whole thing went down.

One summer I found myself in a training routine shimmying down a large rope under a helicopter while it hovered over the ocean. I was onboard with about a half dozen young Marines. But as I watched this unfold expertly, it dawned on me. *Did anybody ask these guys if they could swim?* It was all well and good to pass "sea survival" courses on sea dye, rafts, and smoke flares, but what if the water itself absolutely panicked you?

There are things they don't teach you in your advanced training—and they may be the most essential to your success (or survival).

Mike Kibbe knows this. His first outstanding book, *From Topic to Thesis: A Guide to Theological Research* (2016) helped countless students figure out how to develop a targeted research project and bring it to completion. The rules there were basic, but few explain them to us, and it is left to a coach like Kibbe to make them obvious. His efforts, however, had a wide value as well. For each of us the question is the same: How do you do effective research and "survive" without getting stalled by panic?

The book is light, fun, and deeply serious. Mike drew from his own successful experiences, and he shared them generously with us so that others could learn from his own wins and losses. The insights gained there could not only help with any research but could serve a lifetime of scholarship.

In the present work, Mike has done it again. He is now a young professor with enough years under his belt that he knows what it means to have "three preps" in a semester. He knows the pitfalls of too much preparation and not enough. He knows something about faculty life and faculty despair. And he has weathered these many storms successfully. Mike's simple outline tells you all you need to know before you step into your first class at a college, university, or seminary. First, what do teachers do? What is required as we (a) prepare for class, (b) teach a class, and (c) reflect on the experience afterwards? Here is an avalanche of wisdom that is written in a fun, provocative, challenging way that will guide you through the forest and out the other side. Don't be deceived by his writing style: Mike is writing as if he were with you at Starbucks and telling you secrets. These are the sorts of secrets you'd find yourself writing down. On almost every page you'll say, "Ah! That's me!" because his truths are that universal.

The second half of his treatment is about flourishing. It isn't about how to "survive" under a helicopter over the Atlantic. It

is about swimming smoothly to the raft. About knowing what
your community can and cannot do for you. What tools will
help you succeed. And what the overall aims of our professional endeavors are. It is fine that we become expert teachers
in a classroom. But the reality is we are team members in a
faculty. Our mission is less about a well-done semester; it is
about the mission of the school we serve and knowing our role,
potential, liabilities, and possibilities.

Each of us who serve as deans want more than teachers who
can teach well. We want to see our faculty flourish, find joy, feel
supported, and advance the larger mission. We are not a group
of "work for hire" adjuncts; we are men and women rowing the
same boat in the same direction. Mike here explains what it
means to do well on that boat, what we can expect, and what
we need to do to supplement our lives so that this boat is not
our only reality.

This is a great book that should be in the hands of every new
faculty member. Even experienced faculty will benefit. It will
teach you not simply to figure out your helo headset but teach
you to swim and swim like a pro.

ACKNOWLEDGMENTS

This book truly began when, during my freshman year of college, my father urged me to take education courses. I ignored him, of course, but fifteen years later I finally enrolled in a philosophy of education course with Dr. Mark Jonas at Wheaton College. I was a visiting assistant professor of New Testament at Wheaton that year, my first as a full-time teacher, and I will forever look back at that year as the most formative experience of my professional life. Dr. Jonas (education) and Dr. Gary Burge (New Testament), to whom this book is dedicated, deserve first mention. But it took a village to raise this child, and I would remiss if I did not name at least a few other members of that village: Jeff Bingham (biblical and theological studies), Jill Baumgartner (humanities and theology), Gene Green and Amy Peeler and Lynn Cohick (New Testament), Andy Abernethy (Old Testament), Paul Egeland (education), and Dan Treier (theology). I am indebted to all these and others from the faculty of Wheaton College who mentored me that year, and I can only hope that a little bit of their pedagogical wisdom and Christian virtue has rubbed off on me so that I might go and do likewise.

Being a publisher, I imagine, is a bit like being a student *and* a mentor—not only are you on the receiving end of the initial pedagogical act but you are also committed to strengthening and refining and nurturing and honing the project into something suitable for subsequent performance. Thanks are therefore due to Anna Gissing and the editorial staff of IVP Academic for their work to bring this book to completion.

INTRODUCTION

February 2014. Wheaton, Illinois. (I'm telling you this because you need to know that it's cold outside. And snowing.) I'm chatting with the professor at the front of the room about five minutes before class begins. In five minutes I'll be taking forty students on a journey through 2 Corinthians. I'm a doctoral candidate in New Testament, and this hour in the classroom is the teaching component of my first job interview. Four minutes to go. The students are filing in, and I'm nervously keeping my distance and checking my PowerPoint one more time. I put my Bible on the lectern, along with my notes. Put the Bible on the left and the notes on the right. Switch them back and forth a couple of times to see which arrangement feels better. Check the PowerPoint again. Look for a volunteer to distribute the handout. Wait. The handout. Where's the handout? Not in my bag. Not on the lectern. Not in my hands. (It wouldn't be the first time.) Oh no.

I had been sitting outside the classroom for over an hour (because I'm obsessively early when I'm nervous), and yet, in all that time, it had not occurred to me that my lecture handouts were still sitting on my research carrel desk back in the library. On the other end of campus. Three minutes. Did I mention it's cold outside? I sprint down the hallway, down the steps, up the hill, across campus, into the library, down the stairs, and into my carrel at the end of the last hallway in the basement and grab the pile of handouts that I'd printed two weeks in advance and then forgotten about. (Did I mention I'm obsessively early when I'm nervous?) Simultaneously kicking myself for such a rookie move and laughing at myself because I am, in fact, a rookie, I run back up the stairs, across campus, down the hill, and into the classroom. Go time.

The professor opens our time in prayer while I take deep breaths and wipe the snow off my sports coat. We open our eyes, and I realize I'm in the wrong room. Not literally—had you going there for a moment, didn't I? But *my* room was the one up the hill, across campus, in the basement of the library. My research carrel. My comfort zone. My safe space—I'd spent four years in it, and it was *mine*. (No, graduate students, you don't actually own the library. But you're forgiven for thinking you do after living there for so long.) Now, gasping for air and hoping the snowy-wet copies on the top of my stack of handouts don't end up in the hands of the dean or the search committee chair, I'm in an entirely different—and far less comfortable—space.

I've realized over time just how fitting a moment that was to begin my teaching career. So fitting, in fact, that I relive it on nearly a daily basis. Being inches from total panic because thousands of hours of research and writing have not prevented a single boneheaded move that could ruin everything? Happens all the time. Desperately hoping that there's something in my library that will miraculously plug the gaps in my knowledge before anyone realizes what happened? Only when I'm awake. These feelings aren't *totally* foreign to the graduate student— seminar presentations and (eventually) dissertation defenses, anyone? But the fear of public inadequacy that we've experienced a handful of times is about to become our reality ten, fifteen, maybe twenty hours per week. It's a long way from the carrel to the classroom.

Research carrels are supposed to be quiet. Calm. Private. Focused. Monotonous. Graduate school is a marathon, they say. Just keep moving forward, and eventually you'll see the finish line—who cares how long it takes as long as you get there? Teaching is an endless progression of suicides, one sprint after another, barely enough time in between to catch your breath. The classroom is anything but monotonous, anything but private, anything but quiet. Some of us thrive on the peace, and some thrive on the chaos. Some of us go into graduate school hoping the good times will never end (can I go right from my dissertation defense into a research chair?). Others are counting the days until we are released from the deathly silence of the reference section and free to be with living human beings again. But this book isn't about whether we *want* to go from research to teaching, or for which of the two we find ourselves most suited. Longing for freedom doesn't lessen the shock of experiencing it. Even if you're excited about the change, it's still a cold-wind-in-your-face-while-you-sprint-up-the-hill kind of transition, and the goal of this book is to keep you from slipping on the ice and breaking your neck.

At the time of my dissertation defense, which happened a couple of weeks after the experience described above, I had taught three college courses in person—all of them four-week intensives—as well as a handful of online courses. I wasn't a *complete* novice, but neither was I an experienced teacher, not by a long shot. My first full-time post was a one-year visiting assistant professorship at a liberal arts college, and, I have to say, I was incredibly blessed by that initial appointment. Seven courses, only two preps, wonderful students, and a crowd of mentors who were as invested in my success as I was. All that advantage, and I barely survived. People say that the first year of teaching is overwhelming, and they're not kidding.

Following that year, I received a supposedly long-term appointment at a Bible college that ended after three years when the campus closed. I was given a course release and relative freedom from administrative work for the first year of that appointment, then taught a full load (four or five or six courses per semester) and took on various committee responsibilities for the latter two. This job was somewhat lower on mentoring (more due to limited resources than limited interest) than the previous one, but higher on creative license—I was given quite a lot of space to try new things, make mistakes, and build some courses and programs from the ground up. I also taught twelve different courses in three years, so lesson planning was an ever-present reality.

My third and current job is a tenure-track position, back in the liberal arts world, that includes a major administrative role (speaking of things that graduate school didn't prepare me for!).[1] I've also added a couple of new core courses that

---

[1] See appendix B: "A Plea to Graduate Schools," for some reflections on adjustments graduate programs might make to better prepare students for the carrel-to-classroom transition.

happened to be outside my discipline, so, five years in, new course prep remains a major undertaking. This job comes with even greater freedom than the one before, including not only course design but curriculum design—I've been on the planning committee both for my major (biblical and theological studies) and for our general education core. It's a new university, and therefore a very small one, so my class sizes are much smaller than I'm accustomed to. This is great when it comes to keeping up on grading and developing individual relationships with students, but not so great for delivery of material if you've already got presentation-style mechanisms in place (the lecture and the spiffy keynote just don't work as well when there are three students in the room).

I share a bit of my story here to make two contrasting points: our journeys from research to teaching vary in the details but nonetheless have much in common. "Different masks, but the same flesh underneath," as Tom Clancy put it.[2] You might go straight into a tenure-track or, if you're like most of us these days, you might not. You might have significant administrative responsibilities right away, or you might not. You might be a long-term adjunct or a dual-career part-timer. You might teach partly or predominantly online.[3] And so on. But no matter your personality, no matter your prior experience, no matter the specifics of your situation, the fact is that the move from research to teaching involves a set of challenges for which none of us is ever fully prepared. Hopefully, though, this book can be a helpful and encouraging companion along the way.

---

[2]Tom Clancy, *Debt of Honor* (New York: Berkley, 1995), 156.
[3]As I write this from home during the coronavirus pandemic—well, we're all online faculty at the moment, aren't we?

WHAT TEACHERS MUST DO

The first part of this book is about doing stuff. Teaching, like any other task, involves three phases: preparation, execution, and reflection. Rinse, repeat. First you get ready to do something, then you do it, then you look back on how you did it so you can do it better the next time. I'm going to call these three phases "Before the Classroom," "In the Classroom," and "After the Classroom."

Before the Classroom (Preparation) is about the journey from research to teaching itself. There are four things that are absolutely critical to making the transition. First, *finish the job* you've been working on up to this point: publish your dissertation. Second, *get a mentor*—a *pedagogical* mentor. Find the great teachers at your institution, and apprentice yourself to them. Third, *read a book*. Actually, read lots of books (on teaching). Become a student of your teaching craft just like you were, and will continue to be, of your academic discipline. Fourth, *do the work*. Getting ready to teach requires a lot of content preparation. Good thing you already know how to do that.

In the Classroom (Execution) is about what you do in the classroom. This is where it happens. And if you want what happens in the classroom to be more than you monotonously spoon-feeding information to your students that they will either ignore or forget at their earliest convenience, you might try these five things: First, *tell a story*. Treat every moment of every session of every course as part of a single story, and invite your students into that story. Second, *land the plane*. Graduate students leave students hanging (either because it's fun or because they don't know the answer either). Teachers help them complete the journey. Third, *have a signature*. Be known for something. One specific thing. Talk about that one thing enough that no student could ever fail to associate you with it. Fourth, *take a risk*. Take lots of risks, actually. You're going to fail. You're going to make mistakes. You might as well decide in advance what kind of mistakes you want to learn from in any given scenario. Fifth, *know the center*. What's the *one thing* that matters in a curriculum? In a course? In a session? In an exercise? In an assignment? And how does that one thing at the microlevel feed the one thing at the macrolevel?

After the Classroom (Reflection) is the hardest phase because there's no time. By the time you walk out of one class, it's well past time to start preparing for the next one. But it's also the most important phase because it's how you get better at the job. No one is good at teaching the first time; reflection is a sine qua non of improvement. Reflection is both active and passive. Actively, *find a system*. Decide in advance how you are going to self-evaluate, when you are going to self-evaluate, exactly what sort of things you are going to self-evaluate, and do them. Passively (well, maybe "actively in another direction"!), *take a sabbath*. You are exercising new mental muscles, and muscles only get stronger when they go through healthy cycles of work and rest.

WHAT TEACHERS MUST KNOW

The second part of this book is about knowing stuff. In *The Courage to Teach*, Parker Palmer—stop reading this book and go read that one, if you haven't already, and then come back to your place right here—says that great teaching emerges from the heart of the teacher.[4] But how do you know your own heart?

---

[4]Parker J. Palmer, *The Courage to Teach: Exploring the Inner Landscape of a Teacher's Life*, 10th Anniversary ed. (San Francisco: John Wiley & Sons, 2007).

Self-discovery is unattainable in the abstract. If you want to know who you are as a teacher, you can't meditate your way to enlightenment. You have to go teach. You have to *do* something, in other words, before you can *know* something. But as you *do* the things I've mentioned above (preparation, execution, reflection), you'll come to *know* some vital things about yourself and your classroom.

First, you'll discover your *mission* and your *method*. What are you trying to do in the classroom, and how exactly are you going to get it done? Methods matter. A lot. Lectures are so nineteenth century, we're told—but why are millions of people watching TED talks? A bad discussion is pooled ignorance; a good one is interactive learning. How about flipped classrooms? Subject-centered teaching? There isn't one right way, but there are better and worse ways *for you*.

Second, you'll get to know your *community*. This could mean a lot of things, so I'm going to focus on two groups: your students and your family. And when I say "your students," I mean *your* students. Not the latest research about their peer groups. Not the sociological descriptions of their generation. (Knowing that data won't hurt. But it isn't the same as knowing your actual students.) You have to know *them*. Individually. Their stories. Their passions. Their strengths and weaknesses. And I discuss family in this section because it is so easy to forget about it. I have seen too many academics, including myself at times, make professional decisions with significant and unconsidered implications for our loved ones. Maybe there are jobs out there that have no effect on one's family. Teaching isn't one of them.

Third, you have to know your *limitations*. You can't be a top-tier writer, a well-known speaker, a respected administrator, a sought-after mentor, a successful teacher, and a well-rounded human being at the same time—despite how often you may feel like this is precisely what is being asked of you! It's also worth pointing out that there can be as much danger in actually pulling this off as in trying and failing to do so. You might accomplish enough that people think you're Superman/woman, and, what's worse, you might actually start to believe your own hype.

Fourth, after you've taught for a while, you'll (hopefully) become cognizant of your *power*. Teaching is a dangerous profession—great potential for good, equally great potential for harm. And this isn't just about what you teach in the classroom. Your voice reaches around the world with a click, and with the expansion of your range comes an equal increase in your creative and destructive capabilities.

APPENDIXES

This book ends with three appendixes. The first is about *using your dissertation in the classroom*. You've probably been told that's never going to happen. Wrong. The second is a *plea to graduate schools*. Graduate schools, you are in the business of training teachers. And, if I may be blunt, some of you have some room for improvement in that business. And the third is a list of some of the *great resources on teaching* that are worth buying, reading, and having within arm's length at all times.

PART ONE

WHAT TEACHERS MUST DO

Some years ago, I was apprenticed to a cabinetmaker, and in the transition from one project to the next, he said, "Okay, Mike, this job basically is the same as the last one." Well, it wasn't. Different materials, different dimensions, different everything. But, actually, not different *everything*—there was a fundamental continuity from one job to the next. When he said, "This job is the same as the last one," what he meant was, "The really important lessons about how to make cabinets that you learned on the last job are going to be applied to this job; the only difference is the details." The problem, as he and I found with ever-increasing frustration over the next few weeks, is that I hadn't learned those really important lessons. I'd simply learned how to do that one job.

When you head from the carrel to the classroom, you might have the opposite problem as I did in the cabinet shop—or, more precisely, the same problem from the opposite direction. What little received wisdom exists on this topic tends heavily toward the negative. *Undergraduates don't care about how smart you are. Don't overload them with information just because you think it's interesting. Your dissertation is useless in survey courses.* That sort of thing. You'll hear a lot of "these two are nothing alike" (the opposite of what my boss was saying), and your experience will ring true to that sentiment. But, in fact, as my boss was trying to tell me, there are significant points of overlap that are fundamental to both tasks, and discovery of those common threads are the key to success in both ventures. The classroom is "basically the same" as the research carrel, but it isn't always obvious at what level that's the case.

1

BEFORE THE CLASSROOM

PREPARATION

Four things need to be done in order to get ready for the classroom. I don't mean we complete these tasks before our first teaching experience (that would be nice but not realistic). I mean these are the things we begin to do to signify that we are moving from the carrel to the classroom. Doing these things proclaims, "I am no longer a graduate student!" Because you're not. Even if I am technically still doing doctoral work as I transition to teaching (not recommended but frequently necessary), when I step foot in the classroom, I am not a graduate student. I am a professor. And these are the things that professors do. So I need to do them.

FINISH THE JOB

Whether you move into teaching while still writing your dissertation or after having defended it and submitted the final version, you aren't done until it's published. Be relentless in your pursuit of closure.

Sometimes there is a clear line between "you are a graduate student" and "you are a professor"—you defend your dissertation in the spring, publish it over the summer, and start teaching over the fall. Sometimes. It comes with some frustration to realize that the dissertation isn't actually done when you defend it, isn't actually done when you submit revisions, isn't actually done when the official version comes to rest in the university or seminary library. A dissertation is done when it's *published*. Meaning, I can buy it for an exorbitant amount of money on Amazon right now. Only then is your career as a graduate student truly over. And more often than not, that doesn't happen until well into one's teaching career. It's theoretically possible, of course, to opt out of the publishing lane. They won't take your degree back. But getting that thing in print, and doing so immediately, is crucial for several reasons.

First, and this concerns getting it published quickly, you really don't want to do more research between defending and publishing. The longer you wait, the greater the chance that more literature appears on your topic that will render your project out of date. I have yet to meet anyone who enjoyed starting over with their research after they'd already defended the project. But I have read numerous dissertations whose research was several years behind before they hit the press because they waited too long and then didn't get back up to speed.

Second, your doctoral research is a contribution to the academy as a whole, not only your institution. Unpublished dissertations used to be the norm; if you needed to read one, you could use ProQuest or InterLibrary Loan to access it. Now they're the exception, and the fact is that there are so many published books that an unpublished one just isn't going to get read, so if you want your work to be useful to other scholars, you'd better publish it. A busy researcher just doesn't have time to dig that deep; they'll assume it didn't get published because it didn't deserve to get published.

Third, you need the closure. "Finish the job"—my father used to say that to me constantly. Graduate school is a marathon, and at least in the biblical and theological disciplines, publication is you breaking the tape. Don't quit right before the finish line. Who runs 26.1 miles and stops? Get it done, and get it done right away. This is the absolute final step of your journey, and it's harder to teach when that one little piece of your heart is still in the library.

It's nice, obviously, if you can get this done *before* you start teaching. And if that isn't realistic (and it usually isn't), the challenge becomes getting it done *while* teaching. This isn't the place to walk you through all the hoops; your dissertation committee will be the place to go for advice on publishers, who to contact on the editorial board, etc. Here I simply want to tell you that you can't fully make the transition from student to professor until this is done. If, like most of us, you've started teaching and the publication process isn't complete, make the hard decision to take something off your plate so it can be.[1]

READ A BOOK

Be fanatical in your devotion to pedagogical research.

It's the most obvious thing in the world. You've spent the past few years becoming an expert not simply in a particular academic field but in a particular skill: the skill of learning. More specifically, learning by reading. So start reading. Read

---

[1]Calling these decisions "hard" isn't superfluous. I won't try to give every nuance here because everyone's situation is different. I just want you to hear that as hard as this process can be, it's not as hard as tripping over those loose ends for the rest of your career.

books on teaching, journal articles on teaching, blogs on teaching. Listen to audiobooks on teaching and podcasts on teaching. Go to conference sessions on teaching. Be as much of a researcher in your new vocation as you were in your old one.

Every communicative act has a what and a how—*what* you're going to communicate, and *how* you're going to communicate it. In graduate school we spend the vast majority of our time on the what. Is the argument solid? Is the logic defensible? Is the claim resonant with the data? We ought, in fact, to spend much more of that time on the how—did you know that there are people in your institution who are experts in written communication?[2] But that's a conversation for another day. Right now, the point is that we cannot carry our obsession with the what into the classroom. Graduate supervisors are (sometimes) willing to endure mediocre writing if it is accompanied by brilliant insight. Undergraduate students, not so much. The quality of your what has always been a function of the quality of your research. Now it's time to raise your how to the same standard.

Here's something that should encourage you: literature on teaching is generally more well written than literature in your academic discipline. This shouldn't be a surprise, since, you know, *it's written by professional communicators.* You know those brilliant scholars who just can't seem to get their thoughts well enough in order so that someone who isn't quite so brilliant can understand them? Those people don't write

---

[2]Why do we think that our department is the only one that doesn't need the other departments? If theology faculty roll their eyes when the communications professor says something heterodox in chapel, what do you think the communications faculty are doing when the theology professor publishes yet another unreadable journal article or delivers yet another sure-cure-for-insomnia academic paper?

books on teaching. This doesn't mean all the literature on teaching is good. It means you won't generally feel like pulling your hair out as you try to understand what they're saying in the first place.

If you've got a graduate degree, or are well on your way toward earning one, I don't need to tell you how to research—how to collect sources, analyze arguments, engage dialogue partners, etc. But I will tell you a couple of ways in which you may find pedagogical research to be different than the research you've been doing so far.

First, *emphasize depth over breadth*. That doesn't mean picking one book and devoting ourselves to its insights at the exclusion of all other possibilities. But it does mean we release any expectations about reading everything ever written on anything the way we did in graduate school. No more footnote-stacking, no more spending weeks tracking down that one unpublished German dissertation from the 1930s, no more shelves and shelves of printed journal articles that we'll only read once. Always be on the lookout for new ideas and new ways to implement old ideas, but above all have a set of resources that you return to again and again.[3]

Second, *evaluate your sources via implementation*. You're accustomed to evaluating arguments as you read them. Occasionally a scholarly claim is striking or complex enough that you need some additional time to process it, compare it to some other arguments, etc. Even that can usually be done in a relatively short period of time. But the success of a pedagogical claim is only verifiable via implementation. *You have to go try it.*

---

[3]In appendix C you'll find those books that I return to repeatedly.

If one of your sources says, "Here's something that really works," the only way to validate or invalidate that claim is to go do it in class. Don't just mentally process the claim, don't just make a note in the margin next to the claim. Make a plan to try it in class—and be specific! Decide when and where you are going to try it, actually do that, and then come back to the source and make a note that says, "4.12.18—SysTheo 1—good idea but . . ." or whatever the appropriate comment may be. If it was a good idea but it just needed some tweaking for your context, or simply some more practice, or whatever, implement it again and put another note in the margin: "10.6.19—Hermeneutics— good but slow down." And make sure once you've found the proper space and timing and nuance of the technique that your note includes those details so you can do it again *that way* the next time.

I can hear the protest from all the competent teachers out there: "You can't just create a formula that's going to work the same way every time! It depends on the students, it depends on the material, it depends on the setting. . . ." Of course. I'm not talking about implementing a technique in every session of every class in every semester. The evaluation process includes determining the proper context for implementation; often enough, though, your source will have already addressed that issue. You'll find an idea in a chapter on interactive learning techniques for keeping everyone engaged in a large lecture hall—that idea is only going to be useful to you if you teach a course in a large lecture hall. Another source will suggest a system for evaluating group projects—obviously, you only need that system if you assign any group projects. There are books out there specific to teaching foreign languages, specific to teaching writing, specific to teaching the Bible. If you don't teach those subjects, those books are less likely to be of any use to you. And so on. The point is that you only know if an idea is any good if you try it, and part of trying it is determining when and where and how often to try it.

Third, *read intermittently rather than in big chunks.* My academic research process typically involves (when I am fortunate enough to have it) a large portion of time when all I do is read. Collect sources, scan and print those sources, three-hole punch those sources, and then read those sources. For me, at least, this is the only way to do profitable research in my discipline. The biggest mistake (which I make regularly!) is to start writing too soon. Invariably I get stuck because I simply haven't done enough research.

This isn't entirely misguided when it comes to pedagogical research. Read or listen to a whole bunch of resources on flipped classroom methods, if that's your thing, and think through the relative usefulness of those sources before you implement any of them. For sure, read more than one thing about what a syllabus is and isn't prior to writing any of them. There are a couple of problems though. The first is related to what I said earlier—you evaluate sources *via implementation.* You really can't know if a source is any good without doing something with it in the classroom. Doing all the reading and then deciding which sources are superior before you've tried any of them in real time just isn't going to work.

The second problem is that our classes won't sit on hold until we're ready for them. In graduate school, you could recognize— or be told—that your work was weak in a specific area. And once you identified that weakness, you hit the pause button on your project and sat in that area for as long as it took. When chapter three of my dissertation stunk, I stayed with chapter three until it didn't stink. I didn't go on to chapter four. But in teaching, you don't have that option. In teaching, there is no "pause" button. The next class happens in thirty minutes. Or two hours. Three days *max*. The point is, the bulldog mentality of the graduate researcher just doesn't work here. You need to make a change *now*. So if I have thirty minutes available to me today for pedagogical research, I'm going to spend five minutes triaging—figuring out what really needs to be taken care of right now—and twenty-five minutes going to work on that one problem, reading a blog on that one problem, staying focused in my reading on that one problem. And when my time is up, my time is up. Yes, this is the tyranny of the urgent. Welcome to the classroom. It won't always be this way.

GET A MENTOR (GET SEVERAL OF THEM, ACTUALLY)

Get pedagogical mentors. Your graduate advisor might be a great teacher, but they probably haven't taught the courses you're teaching, to the kinds of students you're teaching, in a long time.

The people who supervise doctoral dissertations are (presumably) scholars of the highest caliber. They've made major contributions to their field and are widely respected voices in the academy around the world. Hopefully, they've been a valuable mentor to you during your graduate studies. But even in that most unusual of situations—your doctoral supervisor teaches undergraduate courses and you get a job at the school where you completed your doctorate—the odds that your scholarly mentor will become your pedagogical mentor are very, very slim. It's time to find some new mentors.

GETTING A MENTOR

Someone with a reputation, both among peers and among students, as an excellent teacher. This isn't hard—just ask around![4] You'll figure out rather quickly that everyone knows who the great teachers are.[5] But ask both students and colleagues; reputation with one group doesn't always translate to the other, and popularity with only one of the two is often a red flag. Names that pop up in both conversations are the ones really worth pursuing.

Someone who knows not only how to teach but how to train teachers. Great teachers are like great performers in any other field (athletes, musicians, etc.). Some are great and have no idea why (think Matt Damon in *Good Will Hunting* trying to explain to his girlfriend why his brain just does things that no one else's brain can do). Some have grasped the reasons for *their* success but don't necessarily know how to translate that into *your* success (think of all the Hall of Fame athletes who failed miserably as coaches). And some not only know what works for them but also know how to inspire and concretely

---

[4]If you teach part-time, or exclusively online, this might sound impossible. Adjuncts often only teach night classes (because they work a day job), so it's harder to find someone willing to stick around for conversation and teaching evaluation. My advice is to *ask*. It might take a little more effort to find someone because the institution probably isn't as officially invested in your development as they would be if you were full-time. So ask, and keep on asking until you get somewhere. If you teach online, you might assume no one is available. But to some degree the opposite is true because all your material is accessible to anyone willing to look at it. And even though many academics look down their noses at online learning (even as we all are pandemically-driven into it!), there are great teachers who are truly invested in digital pedagogy and can serve as wonderful mentors (shout-out to Andrew Beaty of Moody Bible Institute's distance learning).

[5]Gary Burge, in his excellent book *Mapping Your Academic Career*, recommends passing out 3x5 cards to your students and having them list the top five teachers at the institution, then attending class with whoever ranks highest across all your students. Gary M. Burge, *Mapping Your Academic Career: Charting the Course of a Professor's Life* (Downers Grove, IL: IVP Academic, 2015), 70.

train others into doing likewise (think Alicia Keys on *The Voice*). Will Hunting is fun to watch, but he won't make you a better mathematician. Michael Jordan is a fantastic model of how to play the game, but you don't necessarily want him in the gym with you. But a few months being tutored in vocal performance by Alicia Keys? Yes, please. Find the Alicia Keys of teachers on your campus.

Someone who is sufficiently self-reflective to answer the why questions about their own teaching. The most important questions are the why questions. Why did you require that project? Why did you do those two sessions in that order? Why did you change that exam question? Why did you respond that way to that comment in class? Why do you start class with that prompt? Why is *that* one of your course objectives? A great pedagogical mentor always knows the answers to the why questions because everything they do is on purpose.

Someone who pushes you into becoming **you,** *not into becoming* **them.** Remember those graduate school professors who never let their students disagree with them? Identify those teachers, and don't pursue a mentoring relationship with them. Teaching is performing, and no two performers are exactly alike. Mentoring is not cloning. A great mentor knows when to say, "Do as I do," and when to say, "Do as *you* do." This is why you need to know the answers to the why questions. The "do as I do" almost always exists at the why level, not the what level.

Let's say your mentor always begins class with a joke. You can imitate the what—meaning, always start class with a joke. Or you can imitate the why—meaning, find out why they start with a joke and discern the appropriate equivalent for your classroom. Maybe their class occurs early in the morning and most of the students aren't quite awake, so the joke gets them going a little bit. Maybe their class is necessarily intense and heavy (one of my colleagues teaches a course called Biblical Theology of Suffering) and the joke lightens the mood and keeps things from getting too depressing.

If all these things are true for your class, *and you have enough good jokes to tell and are good at delivering them,* you might find it useful to imitate your mentor in the what. But maybe your class isn't early in the morning. Maybe the content isn't particularly dark and intense. Or maybe it is dark and intense, and you want it that way. Maybe you're just not that funny. If any of those apply, starting off with a joke isn't going to work. So imitate your mentor in terms of the why—meaning, start class with something that gets students engaged, fits the mood you want to create for the remainder of the session, and works for you, rather than the what—meaning, telling a joke just because your mentor does. A great mentor doesn't say, "My advice is to start things off with a joke." A great mentor says, "Let's discern what opening gambit is going to take the session in the direction you want it to go."

There will be situations in which the what is worthy of imitation. We naturally gravitate toward mentors that are already somewhat like us in terms of personality, style, etc., and that means a greater degree of appropriate mimicry. My most significant mentors don't lecture, and there's a reciprocal relationship between that and the fact that I don't lecture much. I'm imitating them stylistically, but I also leaned into those masters of the teaching craft because I saw in their style something I wanted for myself. Think about how you chose your scholarly mentors: you pictured yourself becoming the kind of scholar that they already were. Likewise with pedagogical mentors. There's nothing wrong with that! Just be careful that you don't imitate the what until you've understood the why.

Someone who is willing to pour into you and not simply be an occasionally available resource. There are influences and there are mentors. You need both, and you need to appreciate both. An influence is someone from whom you might seek advice on a specific question, or whom you might observe on occasion just to get some additional insight, or whom you respect for one small facet of their pedagogy. You need teachers who play this role for you! But don't mistake the person who is occasionally available to answer questions over coffee or who sits in on your class once or whose videos you've watched for a true mentor. Mentoring is face-to-face. Mentoring is regular and intentional. Mentoring is reciprocal—you'll probably have to take the initiative, but a great mentor leans into you as you lean into them.

Someone who never stops learning. Some teachers swear that we should burn our notes at the end of the semester and start over with each subsequent term. Other teachers change the date at the top of the syllabus each summer and call that "course prep."[6] The second approach never works. The first approach only works if you know your material so well that the only questions left to answer are methodological ones, and you could do the class in your sleep if you had to—so basically never. Actually, it doesn't work even then, because you'll end up making the

---

[6]I have, on occasion, accidentally distributed handouts that have been entirely rewritten *except for* the date at the top.

same pedagogical mistakes year after year if you don't take note of them and remember to avoid them next time around.

You already know that your knowledge of the field is insufficient—you live for those two or three sessions each year that overlap with your specific research interests (more on that later), and the rest of the time you wallow in the insecurity of knowing you don't know nearly enough about the content of the course. If graduate school taught you anything, it should have taught you that learning new content never stops. Likewise pedagogy! You wouldn't have wanted a graduate school mentor who thought they knew everything and didn't need to learn any more—no one should be better described as a "lifelong learner" than a graduate school professor. Likewise for your teaching mentor. Find someone who is always improving, always digging deeper, always honing their skills in the classroom. Then go and do likewise.

Someone who teaches the same courses, or at least the same kind of courses, that you teach. We can learn from any great teacher. We can (and should!) learn from kindergarten teachers, from special education teachers, from football coaches, from choir conductors, from physical therapists, from drill sergeants, from anyone in any environment whose responsibilities include training other people to do something. But we usually learn the most from those whose training environment looks the most like ours. So find a mentor whose classroom situation is comparable to yours on the issues that shape the classroom environment and your teaching approach: size of class (5? 20? 250?), level of class (freshman general education? upper-division elective?), nature of class (lecture? discussion? project-oriented? online?), nature of material (foreign language? text-based?).

Someone who can be brutally honest. People who only say nice things to us don't care about us. Period. And this is partly on us: we can't treat conversations with our teaching mentors like a job interview. We have to show them our warts. We have to invite them to class sessions that stink so we can get better. The mentor exists (in part) to solve problems; they can't do that if we hide our problems. Fortunately, the crucible of dissertation writing and conference presentations has given us some practice in receiving criticism (sometimes delivered graciously, sometimes not).

In my first teaching term, I invited a professor to sit in on one of my classes that wasn't going particularly well. We'd met once or twice already, so I knew something of his style and personality, and I knew that he was going to give it to me straight. After the session we went to my office, and he asked me if I really wanted to know what he thought. A mentor is going to ask that question because they need to know if you are serious about being mentored. The wounds of a friend are faithful![7]

GETTING LOTS OF MENTORS

Have more than one mentor. Their level of involvement will vary, as will your dependence on them in different situations. But if you can find more than one person who meets the above criteria, you'll be that much stronger for it. In that case, here are some things to consider.

Find at least one mentor in the education department, if your institution has one. When I was an undergraduate student in biblical studies, my father (a high school math teacher) urged

---

[7]Mentors: Please don't take this as a license to destroy. Your gifts are ultimately for building up, not tearing down.

me to take an education course. Of course, I ignored him. He said the same thing when I was in seminary, and, naturally, I didn't get it done. Graduate school—you guessed it. I finally heeded his advice after I'd completed my doctorate and obtained a teaching position. I took a philosophy of education course under a colleague in my second semester as a full-time teacher, and it was absolutely transformative. So I'm going to beat this drum as long as you'll let me. If you think it's unnecessary for teachers to be trained as teachers by the people who are trained to train teachers, you might as well stop reading this book.

When it was your primary job to *research* and *produce scholarship*, you apprenticed yourself to those whose vocation it was to train people in those skills. Now it's your job to *teach*. So go apprentice yourself to those whose vocation it is to train people in that skill. I'm not saying only education professors are capable of mentoring you! But I am saying people who have devoted their lives to the classroom as a content area, rather than to another content area within the classroom, are absurdly underappreciated as resources in the pedagogical development of new professors.

Have mentors who represent your student population. The vast majority of my students are not like me, in a hundred different ways. I do not naturally see things from their perspective, so I need mentors who do. I need mentors who can guide my engagement with those students. I need female mentors to help me communicate better with my female students, African American mentors to help me see things from the perspective of my African American students. And so on, and so forth. We can't do this perfectly, of course. But what we can do is (1) identify the perspectives in your classrooms that are most unlike your own, and to which you find yourself least sensitive, and (2) identify the colleagues who best understand those perspectives and are most willing and able to help you to do likewise.

I, as a Caucasian male, am almost always a majority or an advantaged minority in my classroom.[8] As a result, it's always easy to assume that my perspective is the default one and all others are divergences from that default. So what I'm tempted to do is talk to my African American colleague about how to relate to my African American students, and nothing else—as though on every other topic I am not in need of their help. Likewise with my female colleagues: I am tempted to ask them how to connect to my female students, as though that is the sole contribution they could make to my pedagogy. This is certainly untrue! My point here is not that a female mentor (in my case) can only speak into gender-related issues, but that when it comes to gender-related issues, a female mentor is most likely to have the wisdom that I need. Similarly, I am not saying that an African American mentor can only speak into pedagogical issues related to race and ethnicity; rather, I am saying that when I have questions related to ethnic

---

[8]An advantaged minority is a person who, in a particular situation, is numerically in the minority but is able to behave as a majority person might—having their position be the default one, being able to function in line with their identity without fear of reprisal, etc. Missionary kids (as I was) often fit this profile. I was generally able to draw those around me into speaking English, even though that was not the official language of the region. I was able to act like an American might, even if doing so was not appropriate. And if there was any reprisal, I was sufficiently resourced so as to shrug off that reprisal. For example, there were often either implicit or explicit pricing differences for locals and foreigners such as myself. But it didn't matter that I was being charged twice as much, because I could afford it. In my institutions, at least, a majority female student body poses far fewer difficulties for me than a majority male student body does for my female colleagues. That is the essence of an advantaged minority.

minority students, an ethnic minority mentor is most likely to have the answers.

One other word to the teachers who identify as minorities. Your (majority) mentor needs to be the kind of person who will not only speak to you, but, when necessary, speak to others for you. At a former institution of mine, some male students pushed hard against the authority of some female staff members. What happened next was exactly what needed to happen: the senior male professor on campus went nuclear on those students. You might not like that it needed to happen, but it needed to happen. And it wasn't done in a condescending way, as though the female staff members were legitimated by the male professor. It was, rather, the acknowledged authority (the male professor) speaking authoritatively about the legitimate authority of the female staff member. It's called advocacy, and any mentor worth their salt is going to be willing to do this for you if the situation demands it.

Have mentors at various career stages. Call this one the grandma principle. I'm learning, as I raise young children, that sometimes you need a grandma, and sometimes you need a (slightly older) friend. What are the long-term consequences of doing things *this* way? Grandma. When do I start potty-training? Friend. Am I ever going to sleep again? Grandma. How do I settle the earliest sibling conflicts? Friend. Am I a bad parent if I don't use cloth diapers? Grandma. You get the idea.

Think of grandma as the source of perspective, and your friends as the source of practice. Grandma knows that this season won't last forever, and your friends know how to get things done as long as it does. You need regular mentoring from both, but you also need to know which questions to direct to whom. You'll get into trouble if you get it backwards. Let's say I have a six-month-old, and I ask my friend, who has a four-year-old, a two-year-old, and a newborn, if I'll ever sleep again. Their answer: no. Grandma's answer: yes. And grandma is right. But let's say I ask grandma how to get my six-month old to sleep at night. Grandma's answer: they'll figure it out eventually. Friend's answer: Are they using a pacifier? Might they be teething? Do you feed right before putting them down? Is bedtime consistent? Have you let them cry it out at all? Is it sufficiently dark and quiet in the room? Do you use a swaddle? The friend is so much more helpful because they grasp the complexity of your question and they are, from recent experience, very aware of the many practical issues that should be on the table.

The same principle applies to teaching. Sometimes you need the old sage who has seen it all and done it all—how to see beyond the immediate pressures of the job, how to take the long view on dysfunction within the institution, how to stay on a steady path despite the occasional (inevitable) bumps and bruises and detours. But how to find your voice in the classroom? *They don't remember.* How to do new course preps and be on two committees and keep publishing and not lose your family in the process? *They don't remember.* They'll remember whether or not they navigated that season well, and they'll encourage you to maintain that balance and not lose your family, but they won't be able to spell out for you in great detail how to get it done. For those questions you need mentors who were there not long ago. So you need both kinds of mentors, but you also need to know which kinds of questions to ask each of them.

DO THE WORK

You learned in graduate school how to dig deep. Do so for every single class session.

Here's an impossible task: treat every class session like a course unto itself. It depends a bit on the class, but the goal is to know the material well enough to do an entire course on each individual session. Crazy, right? Not as much as you might think. In New Testament Survey, 2 Corinthians gets one session. But I also teach a course on 2 Corinthians. In Systematic Theology, the Atonement gets two sessions. But it wouldn't be strange, would it, to offer an upper-division course on the doctrine of the Atonement? Likewise with Shakespeare in a British Literature course, Southeast Asia in a World History course, and so on.

The *idea* of expanding each session into an entire class isn't so strange (a whole semester on Greek prepositions might sound like a bit much—actually not, though, if there were some particularly motivated students willing to take it). But the *preparation* for that would be insane. A semester's worth of prep for every single week of the term. Any chance you'll pull it off in your first year of teaching? Your tenth year of teaching? Your last year of teaching? Nope. But you'll be closer in year thirty than in year three, and if you make this your goal, you'll never be bored. Always aim for a target that you'll never reach, and you'll always have something to look forward to.[9] I don't mean, of course, that you should perpetually stand under a

---

[9]My Greek students once asked me how close I was to being "fluent" in κοινή Greek. I drew a line segment, with a "zero" point on one end and a "fluency" point on the other. Then I put a mark about 5 percent of the way across from zero to fluency. That's me. And where are they, late in their second semester of Greek Grammar? 2 percent, perhaps? 2.5 percent? The striking thing about that visual is that despite the supposedly vast gap between my knowledge and theirs, we both have a long way to go. As long as I teach Greek, I'll never stop needing to learn more.

cloud of your own inadequacy. Setting unattainable goals actually helps me in this regard because I know they are unattainable from the get-go. So I'm not depressed by my failure to attain them. But I am motivated to keep moving *toward* them (and rightly frustrated when that movement isn't happening), even knowing I'll never get there.

Here's an idea for how this can work in real time. First, choose a session, or a group of sessions, from one of your classes and turn it into a course on paper. Make a syllabus. Identify course objectives, choose textbooks, create lesson plans, etc. Second, do the prep you'd need to do just to barely survive the semester. Read the texts, create the assignments, formulate the broad parameters of the lesson plan. It won't be a fully-developed course—far from it! Third, take that larger set of material that you now have to work with and move backwards. If that whole course had to be crunched down to an hour or two, what would be worth doing from that larger set? The answer isn't "a little bit of everything," or "the recap/overview at the end." It might actually be the very first session you would have done in that class, because that is the session (now redesigned in light of having the whole course mapped out) that is best suited to prepare students to dig more deeply on their own.

The one thing you know how to do when you first move toward the classroom is subject-specific research. You are probably quite good at that because it's all you've done for the past few years. So play to your strengths! Teaching might be far more than content preparation, but it certainly isn't less than that. As you develop your style and your delivery and all those other pedagogical skills, the least you can do is make sure you have a clue what you're talking about every time you enter the classroom.[10] The pressure you felt when it was your turn to present in the graduate seminar or to give a conference paper—that's every day in the classroom. So do the work.

By the way, there's a lesson for both faculty and administration in this with respect to adjunct faculty. Your stereotypical adjunct falls into one of three categories: the graduate student or recently minted PhD trying to break into the game, the retiree who still loves the classroom, and the nonacademic field expert. The last group generally teaches courses that are already very specific to their expertise and the middle group can do pretty much anything, so for them this whole section is a bit of a moot point.

For the first group, however, those who either are still completing their graduate work or have just recently completed it, it can be a nightmare to prep even the bare minimum alongside dissertation writing, multiple part-time jobs, and navigating the job market. So my encouragement to the adjunct, and my plea to the institution, is that folks in this situation be given courses as close to their current research as possible. *Of course* future faculty-hopefuls need to be aiming at competent instruction in the survey courses in their fields. Of course. But they're not there yet, and they're not likely to be in the midst of graduate school. Handing over survey courses (particularly those with large sections) to doctoral candidates is most likely to accomplish the following: (1) significantly delay their completion of

---

[10]One of my seminary professors was a fairly recent PhD graduate who had specialized in the Pauline corpus. The first course I took with him was on the Gospels, and I am struck now—having stood in his shoes years later—how prepared he was. He wasn't terribly dynamic or entertaining, but he was unbelievably well-versed in the material and had enough basic pedagogical skill at that time to communicate things clearly if not eloquently. Knowledge isn't sufficient, but it sure doesn't hurt, especially for younger professors who are still finding themselves pedagogically.

the dissertation, (2) lessen the quality of the course for the students, (3) result in mediocre teaching evaluations that only damage the adjunct faculty member's chances of landing a full-time position down the road. None of these outcomes are advantageous to the institution or the graduate student.

CONCLUSION

Finish the job, read a book, find a mentor, do the work. You know that you can't simply check these four things off the list before entering the classroom. Every time you walk back out of the classroom, these tasks (at least the latter three) will be sitting there waiting for you. But if you can't get them done, you can move them forward, and every step you take toward doing so will have you that much more prepared for the next phase, which is the one you really care about: being in the classroom.

2

IN THE CLASSROOM

EXECUTION

There you are. All nerved up, as ready as you'll ever be. It's go time. Standing outside the room, channeling your inner Lightning McQueen: "I am speed." Actually, not that—has anyone ever told you that graduate students tend to talk *way* too fast? But you know what I mean. You're standing outside the classroom or in front of the classroom waiting for the clock to strike. And hopefully you brought your handouts.

When a person steps in front of a group and does some activity that (1) is highly skilled, (2) requires intense preparation, and (3) is successful only insofar as it captures the attention of the audience, we call that a performance. Musicians, athletes, comedians, actors . . . teachers?

Teacher, thy name is performer. Oh, that more of us would realize this! Denying that we are performing will guarantee a shoddy performance. Some of us still think of ourselves as the mail carrier: drop off the package and move on. As long as it got there, it's not my problem what they do with it. No offense to the mail carrier, but this is not teaching. Do you want

anyone to remember your performance? Do you want the audience to be interested in it, caught up in it, changed by it? Do
you want them to come back and experience it again? Do you
want them to *care*? "They should see the value in the ideas
themselves; I shouldn't have to entertain them." Right. And
whose job is it to enable them to see the value in those ideas?
Whose job is it to put on display for them (perform!) the
implications of those ideas? I'm not talking about entertaining
students. I'm talking about drawing them into the story that
is the intersection of those ideas and your life. You are a performer, and the sooner you think of yourself as a performer
the sooner you'll take the performative elements of your
profession seriously.

For what it's worth, this is more like graduate school than
you might think. We conceive of graduate school as splendid
isolation, with a few climactic moments in the spotlight (conference paper, dissertation defense, etc.), and even then, we
care so much about content and so little about delivery.[1] But
this is wrong in two ways. First, those few spotlight moments
are truly performative. Can you imagine what great actors and
orators would think if they came to our conferences? "Yeah, I'm
definitely worth millions of dollars if this is the average professional speaking gig." Why do we think of those moments as
mere content delivery? If you think I'm exaggerating, just think
about the last time you saw a conference paper that wouldn't
have put your average college senior to sleep. People
supposedly said about George Whitefield, the great preacher,

---

[1]How odd it is that this illness is rarely cured by time in the classroom! I rarely see a
conference presentation that is of such communicative quality that I think, *Oh, that
person must be a great teacher.* Instead, I see people who I know are great teachers
reading their lines like a first-year doctoral student.

that they would listen to him read the phone book. I wouldn't listen to most academics read Mo Willems.

The second problem with the typical perception of graduate school is that every time we put pen to paper—or fingers to keyboard—we are performing. It may be prerecorded instead of in front of a live audience, but we are performing. You, on paper, are vulnerable and exposed before your reader just as you, in person, will be vulnerable and exposed before your students in the classroom. Don't believe me? Just wait until those first reviews of your dissertation come out. If you're still in graduate school, learn to *write* performatively, compellingly, clearly, attractively, eloquently, simply—and you'll have far less trouble *speaking* in those ways when the time comes.[2]

Every performance is an invitation: "Leave your world behind and come into this one for a while!" Think of the last book you read, the last show you watched, the last song you heard. Every one of them creates a space in which some things are true and others are not, some things are possible and others are not, some things are good and others are not. The appeal to you is to abandon your version of reality and live in that one. And, ultimately, every story seeks not only your attention but your allegiance: "When you return to your world, bring this one back with you." This is not a bad thing. It is not an evil conspiracy or some insidious plot by a clever marketer. It is the way things are. No performance is complete without an invitation. We, therefore, as teachers, must know what it is we are

---

[2]I recently spoke with a pastor who is working on his PhD. He is an excellent *speaker*, and a less-than-excellent *writer* (by his own admission). For him, and for others who have spent years in the pulpit prior to graduate school, this logic may simply need to be flipped around. Take what you know about *verbal* communication and apply it to your *written* communication.

inviting our students into, and we must be compelling in our delivery of that invitation.

TELL A STORY

Every course is a season, and every session is an episode.

Consider your favorite sources of digital entertainment: reality TV shows, sitcoms, Marvel movies, fantasy series (e.g., *Game of Thrones, Harry Potter*), etc. There are a million variables in that industry, but no seriously successful product happens without being coherent and compelling at both the micro and macro levels. The *Avengers* franchise is a great example of this—the success of each individual movie is both a function of its internal quality *and* of its relationship to the whole Marvel universe.

Every course, or sequence of courses, works the same way. The implications of this are vast, but here are some things worth thinking about. First, imagine the first episode of each season simply being a thirty-minute roll of the credits.[3] That's what it's like to come to the first day of class and have the professor read the syllabus to you. What is the purpose of the first episode? To make sure there's an audience for the second episode. That's it. One of my mentors likes to say that "the only thing that matters on the first day of class is that when they walk out of your class, the thing that they're talking about is your class." Syllabi can wait. Online learning management systems can wait. Project descriptions, grading scales, all that—it can wait. It can wait until the end of the first session, or even until the second session. Invite them into the story before you tell them about the making of it.

---

[3]Yes, I am aware that movies actually did this just a few decades ago. There's a reason they don't anymore.

Second, each session is an experience unto itself. Each episode is a coherent story: it has a beginning, a middle, and an end. Ending with "I guess we're out of time, we'll pick back up where we left off" is inadequate. Beginning with "picking up where we left off" doesn't work either. And as far as the middle is concerned, this is the great lesson of our digital age: every moment matters. There are too many distractions, too many calls for our attention, too many reasons to tune out whatever the professor is droning on about. Do students need to become more focused learners? Yes. Do students need to discipline themselves to pay attention for long stretches of time because not all that glitters is gold? Absolutely. But we have to give them a reason to do so. Build something that is so tight from beginning to end that to miss a single moment is to undermine the whole experience, and you'll have a lot less Facebook and Instagram in your classroom.[4]

Third, a successful series must stay internally consistent—just check out the online conversations about how *Iron Man 3* relates to *Avengers: Infinity War*. Fans go absolutely insane when the storyline breaks down along the way, and our students are likewise unappreciative if we treat each session as an isolated moment with no build from week to week. To put it in terms used earlier, the answer to the why question about any element of a single class session is always partly a function of the purpose of that class session, and always partly a function of how that class session relates to the whole course.

---

[4]The best person I know at episodic coherence in a monologue setting (rather than a show or movie with dozens of performers and cinematic elements) is the British comedian Michael McIntyre. McIntyre does two things exceptionally well: he never wastes a single breath (sometimes in a two-hour sketch!), and he ties earlier parts of the sketch with later ones in ways that I never see coming but are breathtakingly funny.

Fourth, no profitable show or movie series has ever put the burden of remembering earlier moments in the show entirely on the shoulders of the viewer. If season 4, episode 3 builds on something that happened in season 1, episode 9, but no one remembers it, then season 4, episode 3 is going to flop. And it's not because viewers are lazy or distracted or millennials. If no one remembers episode 1.9 by the time they get to 4.3, it's either because 1.9 wasn't memorable, or because 1.10–4.2 didn't do the work of maintaining that memory. If you say something in week one and it doesn't get mentioned again until week fourteen, is it really the students' fault if they've forgotten it?

Fifth, the story being told in the classroom is part of the whole curriculum, not just the individual course. My Hermeneutics course, for example, is part of a general education sequence that includes Old Testament and New Testament Survey (which I do not teach), and it leads directly into Systematic Theology I and II (which I do teach). Connections to both are important, which means (I know this is a surprise to some of you) that I have to be in regular communication with my colleagues about *their* classes.[5] Do I always agree with my colleagues? Of course not. But I have to be on the same page with them about the overall mission. If I'm a new perspective apologist and my colleague is cofounder of the "Luther Got Justification Right" club, the mission of the university is upheld because our students are learning to think critically, evaluate differing opinions, and handle disagreement with charity. But I need to know that my colleague and I disagree

---

[5]Adjuncts, you're not off the hook for this. Full-timers, you need to keep adjuncts in the communication loops.

so that I can model those virtues when the topic comes up, and so that the big story (the entire undergraduate curriculum) stays on track.

Sixth, keep the momentum. How many times has a great movie spawned an awful sequel (or sequels)? Almost *never* does a franchise hit a home run every time. More often than not, they get worse with every subsequent release (*Predator, Shrek, MiB*). The only thing harder than getting people's attention is keeping it. And it's not simply because part two wasn't as good as part one (it never is), but because part two tried to replicate the wrong elements of part one and missed what really made it special (*Matrix, Star Wars*). Or, perhaps, the directors just saw an easy payday and didn't feel the need to try all that hard (*Iron Man*). Either way, there are two lessons here. First, you can't just nail it on the first day and phone it in the rest of the term. Remember what it's like to be a student in week fourteen of the semester? Tired, burned out, *done*. The worse they're feeling, the more pressure is on you to bring your A-game. Second, make sure you know exactly *why* something went well early in the term. Only then will you be able to maintain that success later on.

LAND THE PLANE

A great movie with a lousy ending is a lousy movie.

Speaking of bringing our A-game from start to finish, I've lost count of how many times I've ended class without really ending it. The content was solid, the delivery was powerful, everyone was clearly with me up until the last moment. But then I said what I thought were the final words, and an awkward silence came over the room as I realized that in order to bring the point home, something else needed to be said. And I didn't have anything left to say. There are a couple of options at this point. Make something up? That doesn't usually go well for me. Repeat what I'd just said and hope it does the work for me the second time around? Yeah, that pretty much never works. Ask if there are any follow-up questions or thoughts or reflections? Once in a while a student rescues me because they've actually thought the topic through more thoroughly than I have, but it's unwise to count on that happening very often.

You have to land the plane. You have to finish the job. Bring it home. Close the deal. You know what I mean. We wish, desperately and foolishly, that our students would simply appreciate the content-thus-far for its own sake. They won't, because—pay attention to this—they care too much to let you off the hook. If they didn't care, they'd be comfortable with you just running out of steam and walking away. They *want* to know what the point is and why it matters.

There are actually two versions of this problem. One is content-based. I teach a session that compares Paul's letter to Philemon with a strikingly similar correspondence from Pliny the Younger (a Roman senator) to a man named Sabinianus, written early in the second century AD. We have a marvelous time talking about socioeconomic hierarchies in the ancient world, the modern world, and on our campus; then we see how Paul subverts those hierarchies. But I struggled for years to say, at the end of the session, exactly what Paul's new vision was beyond, "This is not the way things are done in the Roman Empire." It's like taking someone on a hike but turning back before reaching the summit. Does a trekking guide ever say, "You should just appreciate the trail we've taken for its own sake;

never mind the view from the top"?[6] I couldn't land the plane, and so students walked away confused—they'd tell you it was a great session, but they couldn't tell you what the point was.

Here's where this comes into play for graduate students. Sometimes we fail to land the plane because of our own inferiority. We really don't know the answer to the "real life" question because we haven't lived enough life to have figured that out yet. Other times we fail to land the plane because of our own superiority. We delight in leaving them hanging, in forcing them to swim for themselves, in making them believe that we have the answers and they don't. Of course, what most often happens is that we in fact don't know the answers (option A) but we dangle a carrot as though we do (option B).

So how do we land the plane? For the *content* problem, the only solution is to do what you do best. More research, more thought, more examination until you have a grasp on how the whole argument comes together. One warning on this: it is appropriate, on occasion, to leave them hanging. Not because you don't know where to go next, or because it will make you look smart to know the answers but not reveal them, but because it is pedagogically appropriate to make them either wait until next round, or go home and finish the thought on their own. Pull a *Sopranos* on them—as long as you don't mind getting as much hate mail as HBO did.[7]

For the *application* level, it's a bit more complicated. First, we need to give our students a broader vision of what it means to "use this in real life." The life of the mind is not distinct or

---

[6]Wouldn't you assume, if that were to happen, that the guide didn't actually know how to get to the summit?

[7]There also happens to be a biblical basis for this—check out the endings to Mark, 2 Kings, and Acts.

inferior to the life of the hands and feet. To meditate on a truth, to find oneself overcome by beauty—these are true goods in themselves. Second, we need to give them examples without doing all the work for them. And our examples should sometimes be simply from our own experience and sometimes directed at theirs. Show them how to make the connections. How will they know if no one ever shows them? Third, there will always be sessions for which we simply can't pull this off. Fine. Tell them that! Tell them you've got a powerful truth, but the implications of that truth haven't quite landed for you yet. Tell them what you've tried in terms of application, even if none of those attempts have worked very well. But don't wait until the last second to tell them this. Tell them earlier so that part of the session can be spent collectively moving the ball forward. Ask them for help!

HAVE A SIGNATURE

Be known for something. One *thing. It's the only thing they'll remember.*

Every great performer is known for one thing above everything else. That doesn't mean they can't do anything else, or that they themselves would have identified that one thing as the most important thing about them. It just means that there was something about their performance that stood out, something that their audience remembered, something that *stuck.* Freddy Mercury's mic stick. Ozzie Smith's back flip. Michael Jordan's tongue. Mariah Carey's range. Each of those performers was world class in a host of other (and more important) ways. A signature is not the thing that makes you *great*—it's the thing that makes you *memorable.*

As a teacher, you need to do better than sticking your tongue out or doing a back flip at the beginning of every session. That would certainly be memorable! But your goal isn't simply to make them remember *you*—it's to make them remember *something worth remembering*. When a former student of yours stands up at your funeral and shares the first thing that comes to mind when they think of you in the classroom, what is it going to be?

About half of my Hermeneutics course is spent on the transfiguration of Jesus. When I began teaching that course, my institution had a history of looking down on the history of biblical interpretation ("oh yeah, they used to do that weird allegory stuff; good thing we know better now"), and I wanted to devote a large portion of my course to charitably engaging that history. But I didn't want to lecture through the major hermeneutical trends since the Davidic monarchy or the apostolic period; it's a freshman/sophomore general education course, and no one is going to care. I decided to show them the history rather than telling them the history, and to do so within a single biblical text or cluster of texts, rather than jumping all over the biblical text week to week. So we read Origen, Augustine, John of Damascus, Thomas Aquinas, Oscar Romero, and others, week-by-week, on the transfiguration, and then discussed both their hermeneutical method and their particular take on that tremendous moment in the life of Jesus.

Having done all this, my students (hopefully!) gained an appreciation for a variety of hermeneutical approaches employed within the church at various times and in various places, as well as a sense that the rabbit hole goes far deeper than we imagined, since even in all that time there are questions about the transfiguration that we did not answer. But they also gained an irreversible association between me and the transfiguration— meaning, I have a permanent place in their souls. Every student will forget at least 99 percent of what you tell them or show them. There needs to be 1 percent that sticks, that *one thing*, and you need to decide what you want that *one thing* to be. I want my students to remember that we are called to follow Jesus down the mountain and toward the cross. I want them to laugh every time they think of Peter talking about tents. I want them to look forward to the day when they too will shine like the sun in the kingdom of their heavenly Father (Matt 13:43; 17:2). And if that's all that they retain from my classes thirty years from now, that's not too bad.

You have to be comfortable with your signature. In fact, you have to determine it ahead of time. It can't be something that embarrasses you, or that you wish wasn't all that memorable, or that you don't think was particularly important. I reinforce the transfiguration stereotype, introducing that section of the course with "you've probably heard that I'm obsessed with the transfiguration. Yes, I am." I make fun of myself about it, beginning *almost* every on-campus public speaking oppor- tunity with some joke about how they probably think I'm going to talk about the transfiguration. I find ways to incorporate the transfiguration into informal conversations that almost cer- tainly push the boundaries of exegetical viability. It's not the only thing I talk about, not at all. But it's ubiquitous enough in my classroom to make a lasting impression on even the most disinterested student. If you want your performance to be memorable and meaningful, you need a signature that your au- dience carries with it far beyond the classroom.

TAKE A RISK

Don't take yourself too seriously. Take risks and take responsibility for them when they don't pay off.

Second year of teaching. Fall semester. Greek Grammar I. (My first time teaching that course.) We've worked through adjectival positions in class, so the students know that if the noun has a definite article and the adjective doesn't, the adjective is in predicate position, and if the adjective has the article and the noun doesn't, the adjective is in attributive position. They know that, so of course I should know that, since I taught them. I've put together a worksheet with lots of adjective-noun combinations so they can practice recognizing and translating the various positions. The first three examples are wrong. They are obviously (from the context) supposed to be translated attributively (the good person), but I've written them in predicate position (the person is good). An hour after class, one of my students is in my office. "Are these right?" he asks. Umm, no. No, they're not. "Is this your first time teaching this course?" Umm, yes. Yes, it is.[8]

Imagine making the sort of mistake I've just described in a conference presentation or in a dissertation defense. Your professional life would be over, or at least it would feel that way in the moment. In teaching, this is going to happen. Regularly. Sometimes content mistakes, sometimes (many times!) pedagogical mistakes, sometimes technical mistakes, sometimes communication mistakes, sometimes personal mistakes. I've had to apologize to my students from just about every imaginable angle.[9]

---

[8]Just to be clear, the question wasn't aggressive or disrespectful. It was honest, and I appreciated it. That student and I remain on the best of terms years later.
[9]Not every mistake merits an apology, of course!

Obviously, basic content mistakes like my mishap with the adjectival position worksheet are to be avoided whenever possible! But you need to know that they're going to happen, and when they do, we can't revert to insecure-graduate-student mode and wonder if our life has any purpose and if we should have just stayed home and worked on the farm. Laugh at it, apologize for it, correct it, and move on.

Pedagogical mistakes are another thing. We should go out of our way to make these as often as possible. Take a risk, set yourself up for failure, every single session. Don't take all of these risks every session, of course. But here are some to choose from.

Personal risk. This is the most important risk, and I need to take it every single time I step into the classroom. I am a performer, but not the kind of performer that puts on a mask and becomes someone else in front of the audience. Rather, I am the kind of performer that puts *myself* out there, that puts the most authentic version of *me* in the spotlight to be ignored, criticized, mocked, or misunderstood.[10] Parker Palmer argues that "good teaching comes from the identity and integrity of the teacher."[11] It's *you*. It's you being you, as fully and as appropriately transparent as possible.

This doesn't come easy to many academics. Being our true selves on display is uncomfortable for anyone, and maybe more so for those who love the intellectual life. Horatio Hornblower, the protagonist of C. S. Forester's great series, is early on put to the test by an older and abusive officer. Among other things, he is subjected to

---

[10]See below under "Know Your Style" for more on your self-presentation.
[11]Parker J. Palmer, *The Courage to Teach: Exploring the Inner Landscape of a Teacher's Life*, 10th Anniversary ed. (San Francisco: John Wiley & Sons, 2007), 13.

"The Proceedings of the Inquisition," when Hornblower was submitted to a slow and methodical questioning regarding his home life and his boyhood. Every question had to be answered, on pain of the dirk-scabbard; Hornblower could fence and prevaricate, but he had to answer and sooner or later the relentless questioning would draw from him some simple admission which would rouse a peal of laughter from his audience. Heaven knows that in Hornblower's lonely childhood there was nothing to be ashamed of, but boys are odd creatures, especially reticent ones like Hornblower, and are ashamed of things no one else would think twice about. The ordeal would leave him weak and sick; someone less solemn might have clowned his way out of his difficulties and even into popular favour, but Hornblower at seventeen was too ponderous a person to clown.[12]

"Too ponderous a person to clown" when one's inner self is put on display. Forester might well have been talking about many graduate students and early-career academics. The greatest risk of all is being ourselves—not inappropriately, not unprofessionally, but honestly.

Session risk. Ask five teachers how many times they have to teach a course before the constant panic goes away, and you'll get five different answers. But they'll all have an answer—it will happen! At some point, you'll have taught a course enough times that you'll feel like you know what you're doing. This is a wonderful and dangerous moment because it brings with it the temptation to stop risking, and when you stop risking, you'll get bored and lazy and your students will know it.

---

[12]C. S. Forester, *Mr. Midshipman Hornblower* (New York: Back Bay Books, 1998), 15.

Here's a simple way to avoid boredom: every semester, choose one session from your "I've got this one down" class and change it. Revamp your presentation of the same topic, change the topic altogether, switch from a lecture to a discussion, or vice versa, do a bunch of research on the topic (come on, former grad students—you *know* there's plenty to work with here!). Reconceive the beginning, the middle, or the end. Take one minor point and go nuts tweaking it. Get a communications colleague to come in and work with you on intonation, or nonverbal cues like gestures or facial expressions. Invite a former student to team-teach it with you and see how their approach reflects what you did when they were in the class.

The all-time greats in every profession constantly find new ways to challenge themselves and to analyze their performance at levels unimaginable to their colleagues. Ted Williams, doing the kinds of statistical analysis on pitchers in the 1940s that today's stat geeks with their advanced algorithms, HD replay, and digital analysis are just catching up to. Hakeem Olajuwon, breaking down low-post footwork at levels of detail you and I can't see even in slow motion. If you think you've nailed it in a particular session, you're wrong. You just haven't looked closely enough. So take risks by trying new things even if what you've done in the past has been pretty good.

Environmental risk. I'm pretty sure you have to be a bit of a control freak to be an academic. You have to be a little obsessive about things and a little intense about your environment being just the way you want it. Pedagogically, this translates into "this is *my* classroom and every molecule in the room is controlled by *me*. *I* set the stage, *I* guide the 'conversation,' and *I* determine the outcomes in advance."

An environmental risk means relinquishing control of the room at one of two levels: the process and the outcome. To relinquish control of the process means we invite students to be part of the story. We don't hide behind our lecterns, we don't do all the talking, we don't treat our students as merely an audience to our performance, but rather as performers themselves. The comedian that brings audience members up on stage, the musician that asks for random notes from the audience before composing a song in front of them comprised of those notes—this is how you risk the environment.[13] There's always a chance that the joke will flop because of how the audience member handles the situation. But how awesome is it when it works! A good performer predetermines everything. A great performer doesn't have to. So give your students ownership of the room. Let them speak. Let them discuss. Let them ask. Let them push back. Let them decide elements of the arrangement of the room, the lighting, the mood, the media outlets, the sequence of events, even the topics of conversation, anything you can to help them see that this is their story, not just yours.

To relinquish control of the outcome is a different thing than relinquishing control of the process. Risking the outcome is precisely what the great performers do *not* do. You can throw every imaginable variable at them, you can cause all kinds of interference, you can keep them constantly guessing, but in the end they still take over the show. Sprain an ankle in the biggest

---

[13]Here's Ben Folds doing a spontaneous orchestral composition, for example: www .youtube.com/watch?v=BytUY_AwTUs.

game of your life? Tape it up tighter and score forty-three points anyway.[14] Power goes out in the middle of your concert? Sing a cappella and invite the audience to join you.[15] The best performers are the ones who can take any unexpected twist and maneuver it toward their original goal.[16]

A friend of mine teaches exclusively from a discussion-based model. No lecturing whatsoever. So he risks at the procedural level all the time—and yet the outcome of each class session is absolutely determined in advance. He knows the questions he's going to ask, he knows the answers they're going to give, he knows the objections or side issues they're going to raise and how he's going to respond when they do, and he knows the path they're going to take from the beginning to the end of class. Students are indeed part of the conversation and part of the story, but the outcome is 100 percent foreordained. Part of this is simply the wisdom that comes from having posed the same question to students year after year—patterns emerge concerning how the discussion will unfold. Part of it is intentional—the questions are designed to evoke certain responses, which in turn lead to the next set of questions that are likewise geared toward certain outcomes, and so forth.[17]

---

[14]Isiah Thomas, Game Six of the NBA Finals (June 19, 1988).

[15]Justin Bieber, Apollo Theater (June 18, 2012).

[16]In military terms, it's important to distinguish between thinking of your students as subordinates and thinking of them as the enemy (this might seem obvious—but you've probably seen teachers who didn't quite get the distinction). In war, you never risk the process on purpose. You control every level of the engagement whenever possible. But in training, you teach your soldiers that they won't always control the process, and that they need to be able to adjust as necessary in the moment. So you lead them through the risk of not controlling the process in order to make sure that they can still control the outcome.

[17]This is the true Socratic method as one finds it in Plato's *Republic*—a sequence of questions whose answers are predetermined by the questioner.

So—should we ever risk the outcome? Should we ever come into class thinking, *I really don't know where this is going to end up, and that's a good thing,* or *I want to end up here, but there are factors beyond my control that might prevent us from doing so and that's okay*? Possibly, yes. But it depends on two factors.

First, what do we mean by "outcome"? In pedagogical terms, an outcome is what we want students to gain from the course or the session. As a general rule, then, no, we don't release control of the outcome. The outcome is the whole point. The outcome is the reason why we're in the classroom in the first place. It's the single nonnegotiable of the whole experience.

Let's say I take my kids bowling. It isn't necessarily the case that bowling is the desired outcome. It might be that "having fun with my kids" is the nonnegotiable. So if I get to the bowling alley and spend the whole time eating popcorn and playing arcade games and talking, I've still achieved my outcome. On the other hand, my outcome might have been "teaching my kids to bowl." In that case, I'd better get my shoes, get my lane, and get bowling. In the classroom, you might think that your outcome is "learn this set of information," in which case anything that keeps you from learning that set of information is a risk you're not going to take. But you might also decide that the real nonnegotiable isn't that set of information but rather a formative encounter with a primary text, or a certain conversation among students. If that's the case, who cares exactly what information they come away with as long as the encounter or the conversation took place? So what might look like risking your outcome isn't; you just had a different outcome than what someone may have guessed.

The second factor is your level of confidence in the appropri-
ateness of that outcome. Maybe this is a new prep for you, and
you still don't know how the whole story coheres. So it's hard
to know for sure if your outcome for any given week is the right
one or not. In that case, by all means be willing to risk the
outcome if you can see, as the session goes along, things moving
in a new direction that could conceivably be better than the
one you had originally determined.[18] So risk your outcome—
that is, let the communal performance of the classroom move
in a direction that you had not foreseen and that likely pre-
cludes the accomplishment of your original goals, if you can
judge in the moment that this will lead to superior outcomes.
But keep in mind that your purpose of doing so is to gain clarity
on your outcomes. Next semester, or next year, or even next
hour (if you have multiple sections of the course simultaneously), you should have learned something from your risk-
taking experience. If you've learned that your original outcome
was no good, don't even aim for it next time. If the risk failed, if
what actually happened in class was disastrous, make sure you
don't let it happen again. And as you teach that session repeatedly, you'll get closer and closer to an outcome that will
become less and less negotiable.

Stylistic risk. We all have preferred approaches. Personally, I
don't like lecturing. This is partly because of the voluminous
research that demonstrates beyond any reasonable doubt that
simply listening to someone talk for hours on end isn't the best
way to learn. It's partly because my greatest joy as a teacher is

---

[18]When we come into class having absolutely no idea what the goal is, that's not called
being a rookie. That's called not doing the job. There has to be an end in mind, even
if we call an audible halfway through the course and change it.

to hear students speak truth, and they can only do that if I let them speak. It's not, I should mention, simply because I've had bad experiences with lecturers. Of course I've had bad experiences with lecturers! But I've had equally bad experiences with discussion groups and every other kind of teaching model out there. And the majority of my professors over the years have been lecturers, and many of them were *good* lecturers. I've simply found that I can't replicate what they did, and at this point, I don't really want to.

The problem is that the best way to teach any given set of information is relative to several factors: the nature of that information, the size of the class, the age of the students, the length of the session, the time of day, the time of year, and, *way* down the list in importance, the personal preference of the teacher. For example: my very first teaching experience was a New Testament elective, covering 1 John and James, to three students, from 6:00–10:00 p.m. You are out of your mind if you think you're going to stand behind a podium and lecture your way through that course. On the other hand, I taught a course not long ago on the transfiguration that had forty-seven students and ran in fifty-five-minute sections. It's *really* hard to have a quality discussion in fifty-five minutes with forty-seven students in the room. I tried, and it didn't go very well. The best discussion-style teachers I've seen tell me forty students is their max, and I believe them![19]

Those who—like me—tend more toward interactive learning environments need to be willing to lecture if the occasion demands it. It might be that there are simply too many

---

[19]A "quality" discussion is one in which *everyone* in the room is part of it. Anyone can have a discussion with the three students in the front row while everyone else watches, and at that point it doesn't matter if "everyone else" means five students or five hundred students.

people in the room or that time is too short. It might be the nature of the material. The vast majority of my Hermeneutics sessions, for example, are discussion based. But on one occasion I want to tell my students a story that begins in Exodus, includes nearly the whole of Deuteronomy and Jeremiah, stops briefly in Ezekiel, and climaxes in 2 Corinthians 3—one of the more challenging texts in the New Testament. You can't, in any reasonable amount of time, discuss your way through this material. So when we get to this session (usually about nine or ten weeks into the semester), I take a risk. I tell my students at the beginning of the day what I'm going to do and why. But it's still a risk because by now they are well-accustomed to participating in the conversation, and it's a bit jarring for them to simply sit there for ninety minutes listening and taking notes. And the risk doesn't always pay off. That might be because I don't nail the delivery. It might be because a particular group of students hasn't been adequately trained in learning from lectures. It might be a trust issue—I ask them at the beginning to trust that this is going to be worth it, and if I haven't earned that trust, or if it doesn't end up being worth it, I've actually diminished my chances of really accomplishing something with them in the weeks to come, especially if I want to lecture again later on.

The best time to take a style risk is when you've got the basic content of a session down cold, but the delivery doesn't seem to be working. You know the material forward and backward, but your students aren't catching on. In this situation you can afford to switch things up without sinking the whole ship because you can always lecture-rescue the class from a complete disaster, and because you can afford the time it takes to rearrange the lesson because you don't need to review the material itself.

Expectation risk. We don't know what our students are capable of. But every semester, we're going to ask them to do things anyway. That's a risk. To some degree, it's a risk no matter what—even if we've assigned a project twenty times before, you don't know if this particular group can pull it off. But I'd encourage you to push the envelope a little more than that: invite your students to do something that you don't know they can do because you've never asked them to do it before.

Expectation risk could run in a few different directions. I might need to raise the bar in terms of quantity—as long as it doesn't turn into busywork. Busywork is work that has no outcome other than filling the gradebook. Busywork is work that doesn't contribute to the overall objectives of the course. And it's important to realize that busywork is as much a matter of perception as of reality. If a student doesn't understand how an assignment contributes to the objectives of the course, to them, it is busywork. *We have to communicate not only the what but also the why of every expectation.*

You might also need to raise the bar in terms of quality. Let me rephrase that: you absolutely need to raise the bar in terms of quality. But don't become a fiat professor—the kind of teacher that thinks all they need to say to their students is "go do X," and X will be done. It doesn't work like that. If I want a higher quality of writing in my course, for example, the bar goes up for me as much as for them. Better writing is rewriting (heard that one before?), and that means editing. *By me.* More drafts, more feedback, more time and energy on my part. I can't ask of them what I'm not willing to do myself.

Know the center. Every great performance has a center, and every element of the performance relates in some way to that center. If it doesn't, it shouldn't be there. It's the ultimate answer to all the why questions. Think of it like a Sierpinski triangle. (Sorry—my dad was a math teacher.) A Sierpinski triangle is an infinitely subdividable triangle whose subsets are identical to the whole (i.e., a fractal).

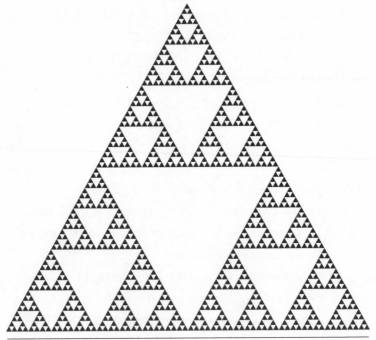

Figure 1. Sierpinski Triangle

Ignore the big (inverted triangular) blank space in the middle, and notice how the three sections (right, left, and top) are identical to the whole thing. Then, within each of those sections, do that again. And again. That's a fractal—the picture is identical no matter how far you zoom in or out.

This is a wonderful image of what's "basically the same" (remember the cabinet shop?) about graduate school and teaching. Start with a dissertation. One big triangle, one primary point at the top. That's your thesis. If you don't have one, you don't have a dissertation. But the dissertation is also comprised of individual chapters, each of which has its own singular point on which the thesis is built. And each subsection of each chapter does the same. And so on, and so forth. The coherence of each layer is a function of (1) the relationship between the one main point and all the other points on which it is constructed, and (2) the relationship between each of those points and the other points on which they are constructed.

There are three questions you can ask when you look at a dissertation in this way. (In a moment, we'll come to these same questions concerning your teaching.) First, does every single piece of the whole contribute to that one point at the top? Thesis writing 101: *no data dumps*. Your supervisor doesn't want to read a regurgitation of *information*. They need you to make an *argument*.[20] And that argument is the one point at the top of the Sierpinski triangle toward which every single chapter, section, paragraph, sentence, phrase, and word is oriented.

Second, how far in should I zoom? Here a communicative act like a dissertation isn't quite like the mathematical construct. You can zoom in forever on a true Sierpinski triangle. But part of the communicative act is the decision to know when to stop—how much information is enough, and how much is too much? This decision relates to time factors (when

---

[20]Most of you reading this book won't need instruction on this point, but if you do, check out Michael Kibbe, *From Topic to Thesis: A Guide to Theological Research* (Downers Grove, IL: IVP Academic, 2016).

do I plan on graduating?), relevance factors (does that word/ phrase/sentence/paragraph/section/chapter *really* contribute to the argument?), and shared basis (does my target audience already know and assume that I know that piece of information?). Bottom line: How far down do you have to go to make your one single point to your particular audience? Go that far and not an inch farther.

Third, does the whole thing fit together? It isn't just that a chapter has to contribute to the thesis. It's that a chapter has to contribute to the thesis in proper relation to the chapter before it and the chapter after it. In writing, you first come up with an idea and then a whole slew of words to express that idea. But each word is evaluated not only in its relation to that idea but in relation to the sentence in which it falls. The "right word" has to be the right word for that sentence. So now you have a sentence. And it might be a brilliant sentence, but it's only the right sentence if it is the right sentence for that paragraph. Do that a few times, and now you have a paragraph. But that paragraph is only the right paragraph if it's the right paragraph for that section. You get the point. At every level, *coherence* is key. It's the same principle as the "tell a story" point I made earlier: a beautiful scene is still the wrong scene if it doesn't fit the scene before it and the scene after it.

Now ask the same three questions of your teaching. First, does every single piece of the whole contribute to that one point at the top? Every set and subset (course, session, in-class exercise, homework assignment) should have a single point. And that point is an *argument*, not a *fact*, not a *set of information*. Just as data for data's sake had no place in the dissertation, *coverage for coverage's sake* has no place in the classroom. "Coverage" is overrated. Your primary task is not to cover a certain set of material. Your primary task is to make an argument. Does your class include information to cover? Of course it does. Facts, dates, definitions, sequences, formulae, procedures, etc. But there is an infinite number of such items at play, and your decisions regarding which ones to incorporate must be driven by something else, and that something is your argument. Coverage is not the ultimate goal. The ultimate goal is to convince your students of some reality and its importance.

This is true even in courses that are traditionally content-oriented. Bible Survey classes, for example: memorize the books of the New Testament, their authors, dates, recipients, and outlines. Regurgitate that information on a Scantron final exam. It's so boring. Stop it. No one cares. Is that information important? Sure it is. But it's important as a means to an end, not as an end in itself. Show your students the end. They won't care about the means if you don't show them the end. It is practically holy writ that the purpose of a New Testament Survey course is to "cover" the basic information set regarding each book of the New Testament. I respectfully disagree. The purpose of a New Testament Survey course is to convince students that the New Testament, in whole and in part and in intricate relation to the Old Testament, is the textual center of the universe. I don't care if my students can outline the book of Romans. I care that Romans has taken hold of them. I care that they are captivated by it. And I don't necessarily need to "cover" all sixteen chapters in order to accomplish that. Blow their minds and change their lives with Romans 1, and they'll read the rest of the letter on their own and be rightly oriented toward doing so.

Thesis-driven (rather than topic-driven) teaching also works in course sequences where later courses are specifically built on the content of earlier courses. If I teach Greek Grammar, and someone else teaches Greek Exegesis, the other professor has a right to expect certain content to be consistently communicated in my classes. If my classes are systematically followed by an equivalency or aptitude test of some kind, I must—bound by faithfulness to those tests—include certain content. But if my primary goal for Greek Grammar II becomes "the student will memorize the forms so as not to make a fool of themselves in Greek Exegesis I," I've failed as a teacher. Are we going to memorize lots of forms in Greek Grammar, and will doing so save them much humiliation in Greek Exegesis? Absolutely. But that is not what drives Greek Grammar. What drives Greek Grammar (in my case) is the claim that κοινή Greek, as found in the New Testament, is a language. Not a code, not a weird linguistic entity that plays by a completely different set of rules than every other language out there. It's a regular old language. And every single thing we do in Greek Grammar should be driven by that one argument. The content we learn. The examples I give. The interpretive skills I demonstrate. All of it.

Second question: How far in should I zoom? As with the dissertation, time constraints and audience are determinative. And this is where I really need to know my students (more on that later) and I really need to know the curriculum. If I don't know what was taught in Verbal Communication I, I'll have a hard time knowing what to do in Verbal Communication II. I'll get that look from students that says, "We already know this; can we move on?"

On the other hand, and this is probably a common sin among teachers fresh out of graduate school, I sometimes shoot way over their heads, and no one will really understand anything because I didn't show my work on their level. Remember the teacher who just *got* physics and so looked at a complex equation and gave you the answer, without any intermediary steps, as though it were obvious? And to you, it wasn't obvious at all. But that's you, now. The basic facts and practices of your discipline are now so intuitive for you that you've forgotten what it's like *not* to understand them.

There's no magic bullet for this problem. Your best way forward is simply trial and error. But to learn from your errors, you'll need to keep a couple of things in mind. First, a good evaluation (quiz, exam, paper, etc.) is an evaluation of your teaching, not simply of their learning. If they're not getting it, it's in part because you didn't give it to them on their level. Second, practice on people who are less educated than your students. If my first-grader at home can get it, my college students can get it. Third, don't be afraid to ask them as you go along. And don't ask them—I'm frequently guilty of this— "does this make sense?" Chances are, you're not going to get an honest or accurate answer. Ask them a specific question that forces them to demonstrate whether or not they've understood what you've communicated. Fourth, let their questions be an indication of how close you are to the sweet spot. You can tell by the nature of the question whether they are leaning backward (I don't get it) or leaning forward (I get it, and now I'm thinking about an implication that we haven't talked about yet).

Third question: Does the whole thing fit together? I can't say this enough: every word, every activity, every project, every assignment, every discussion point, every *everything*—they all point to the one main point but also cohere with what's right around them. There's a time and a place for "Prof's five random reflections on the reading," but it is a time and place of your choosing that actually coheres with the outcomes of the course and the session. And don't forget that your outcome may be skill-related rather than content-related. That is, your argument for the day may be "the one thing from the reading that you need to wrestle with is X." But it might be, on the other hand, "The goal today is to practice critical engagement with narrative portrayals of the hero." In this case, "five random reflections on the reading" works just fine if those reflections are all pointing, directly or indirectly, toward a critical engagement with the narrative portrayal of the hero. Which of these outcomes is appropriate for that session depends, again, on the role that session plays in the entire course. *Coherence* is key, at both micro and macro levels.

So that should encourage you: the singular focus of your graduate thesis or dissertation translates into the classroom. But there's more good news! There are three benefits that you will accrue by shifting your classroom focus from "here's the stuff I should probably cover" to "here's the one argument I'm going to make."

First, you get to play to your strengths. I don't just mean your strengths as someone accustomed to making focused arguments. I mean your strengths within the material itself. After I completed my doctorate, I was hired to teach New Testament Survey at Wheaton College. (Actually, Wheaton calls it New Testament Literature and Interpretation in part to avoid the "coverage" connotations of a survey course.) I had written my dissertation on Hebrews and was, predictably, drowning in the study of the other twenty-six books of the New Testament in preparation for my classes. But the senior New Testament faculty at Wheaton encouraged me *not* to try to cover all twenty-seven books. Why? Because they didn't believe in simply "covering" the material and because they believed my job was to give the students the best possible engagement with the New Testament. So, for example, one section of the course met for two hours at a time, twice each week. Pretty typical. And in one of those weeks, I had a choice to make: I could spend two hours in the Pastoral Epistles and two hours in Hebrews, or I could skip the Pastoral Epistles and spend four hours in Hebrews. Since I wrote my dissertation on Hebrews, and since I'd never done any serious work in the Pastoral Epistles, and since I had in my back pocket a handful of ways Hebrews can change your life and none at all for the Pastoral Epistles, I chose the latter option. And the class was indisputably better for it.

The second benefit to teaching around an argument instead of an information set is that every session forces students to stay engaged. People check in and check out of a data stream. But if there's a single coherent argument that tracks from the opening moments to the closing bell, you either get all of it or you get none of it, and students are going to want to get all of it (if you've introduced the final destination in a compelling way, of course!). If we habituate our students to know the whole thing is going somewhere, they're more likely to stick around for the entire journey.

Third, and I know I'm going against a lot of received wisdom here, there's no reason why you can't get technical publications out of an undergraduate class session. I don't mean that you simply lecture through your most recent journal article! I mean that if a two-hour class session is centered around a significant argument related to your material, and you have several dozen of these sessions each term, odds are good that somewhere in the pile is a scholarly contribution. In fact, it's been a long time since I've published anything that didn't start, or at least make significant progress, as an undergraduate class session. I still do plenty of research on the side that doesn't get mentioned in class. And the session itself may still be a discussion rather than a lecture (though these sessions are often the most suitable for a lecture). And even if it's a lecture, you still have a lot of work to do to shape the material into a scholarly contribution—two different audiences, contexts, etc. But the heart of a scholarly contribution is an argument, and you can begin to form those arguments in the classroom.

Most of your sessions will be old hat to the average scholar. I have absolutely nothing to say about Greek adjectives that every other Greek teacher, and certainly every true expert in the language, doesn't already know. And that's a good thing! If I try to break new ground in every session, I am going to be off base more often than not. But even if you aren't doing anything new in terms of content, there's always a chance you've made a pedagogical contribution. One of my recent articles is a short piece with *Didaktikos*, a publication devoted to teaching Bible and theology.[21] It stems from one of my Hermeneutics sessions on the Gospel of Mark, and it says nothing at all about Mark that should surprise any New Testament scholar. The essay is

---

[21]Michael H. Kibbe, "I Want to Be Like Mark," *Didaktikos* 3.1 (2019): 26-29.

about *teaching* the Gospel of Mark and (hopefully) does make a small contribution in that area. So even sessions that are substantively mundane (to the experts) can be pedagogically innovative and worthy of that broader audience.

Choices are unavoidable when you prepare to teach and actually teach. The possibilities are endless, the realities are not. You need a consistent mechanism for deciding what stays and what goes—you need a point at the top of your triangle toward which every pedagogical act is oriented. If you don't have one, you'd better figure it out pretty darn quick. Otherwise you can't prepare the class (because you don't have a goal in mind), you can't execute the class (because you don't know what to do or not do in the moment), and you can't evaluate the class (if you don't have a target to hit, you won't be able to look back and see if you hit it). So find your center and be relentless in your movement toward it.

3

AFTER THE CLASSROOM

REFLECTION

The emotional state of a teacher right after class is like that of any other performer: elation, exhaustion, depression—you walk off stage with that "my brain and heart are so full right now I think I'm going to explode" look on your face. Sometimes you feel like you could keep going all night; other times you'd like to curl up and die, or at least quit and do something else. I can hardly say it better than Parker Palmer:

> I am a teacher at heart, and there are moments in the classroom when I can hardly hold the joy. When my students and I discover uncharted territory to explore, when the pathway out of the thicket opens up before us, when our experience is illumined by the lightning-life of the mind—then teaching is the finest work I know.
>
> But at other moments, the classroom is so lifeless or painful or confused—and I am so powerless to do anything about it—that my claim to be a teacher seems to be a transparent sham. . . . What a fool I was to imagine that I had mastered this occult art—harder to divine

than tea leaves and impossible for mortals to do even passably well![1]

Can you relate? Good. Both of those feelings are legitimate and normal and healthy. It's when we feel neither that we might be in trouble. The greatest danger to a teacher is not failure but apathy. I have a note in my office to myself that I wrote following a particularly bad day in the classroom: "When I stop being this frustrated about stinking at my job, it's time to quit." *That's* when it's time to quit. Not because I had a bad day but because I had a bad day *and didn't care enough to do something about it.*

This is the "do something about it" section. Class is over. Now what? Two things: evaluation and rest. Two things that I'll never get around to if I don't just make it happen. For evaluation, I need a system. I need a plan, and I need to stick to that plan.[2] And for rest, you need more than a day on the couch. You need a sabbath. You need a regular time during which you walk away from the classroom and the campus to be with the God whose constancy will keep you during the inevitable mood swings of the professoriate.

FIND A SYSTEM

"If you don't write it down, it never happened."[3]

The image of the graduate student in heavenly (or hellish) isolation, pouring over ancient manuscripts or gazing unceasingly

---

[1] Parker J. Palmer, *The Courage to Teach: Exploring the Inner Landscape of a Teacher's Life*, 10th Anniversary ed. (San Francisco: John Wiley & Sons, 2007), 1-2.

[2] I could fill another book with my own failures in this respect—stories of making the same mistake two, or three, or four times because I didn't follow my evaluation-and-correction plan after the first time.

[3] Tom Clancy, *Debt of Honor* (New York: Berkley, 1995), 630.

into a microscope, applying their tremendous-yet-untapped intellectual prowess to one of the world's great quandaries (cue your favorite "what my friends/parents/spouse/I think I do" meme) is a myth. Graduate school is complicated. Seminar papers, teaching/research assistant responsibilities, conference plans,[4] publishing possibilities, part-time employment, family rhythms, comps, and, oh yeah, writing a dissertation while keeping at least one eye on the job market. It's a marathon, all right, but less the "find your stride and turn your brain off for eight miles at a time" kind and more the "follow the switchbacks up and down the mountain and keep your eyes peeled for snakes" kind.

But for all that complexity, there are many days in graduate school when you arrive at your carrel/office/favorite coffee shop and say, "Today's task is to work on chapter (three). Nothing else. It will be a successful day if I stay focused on that one task from now to quitting time." There are no days like that in the classroom. None. All that stamina you developed in graduate school, where you could actually focus on one task for eight or ten or twelve hours straight? The only time you'll use that skill is at the end of the semester when you've got nothing on your desk but grading—and if you can grade for eight or ten or twelve hours straight, well, you're a better person than I am. For the most part, you'll be lucky to devote more than a couple of hours to any given task without interruption. You're going to

---

[4]In my field, graduate students are sometimes required to submit the whole of a potential conference paper rather than a mere abstract, so the timeline looks something like this: write a seminar paper or dissertation chapter (August–December), revise and submit to the appropriate conference section (January–March), forget all about it and move on to the next thing (April–October), frantically review and try to remember why you wrote what you wrote a year ago before you present at the conference (November). It's a hard rhythm for a graduate student who has moved on to the next chapter or seminar long before the conference presentation actually happens.

cycle constantly between course prep, administrative tasks, grading, student interaction, teaching, research, writing, and various off-campus professional responsibilities.

My perspective on this is shaped by my own situation. I teach at a small school where faculty-student relationships are informal, where the administration and faculty all have offices down the same hallway, where my own office is ten feet from the academic front desk. We technically have office hours, but for the most part we just walk up and down the hall and talk to each other. This setup has strengths and weaknesses, obviously, as will whatever situation you find yourself in. Maybe you've got more isolation and formality, maybe you've got less. Lots of variables here, and there's no one right way to handle it. It depends partly on you, partly on your institutional ethos, partly on the time of year, partly on the unpredictability of life. What is most important is that you have a system, and that you are constantly balancing between sticking to your guns and adjusting to the needs of the occasion.

The need for a system applies to the whole of faculty life, but I'm discussing it here, in the context of reflecting on our time in the classroom. Reflection is the single easiest thing to lose track of in the chaos of the semester. Reflection and self-evaluation will almost never feel urgent. It is rarely quantifiable, and it is rarely necessary (in the sense that it must be done today or some concrete thing will fail tomorrow). There will always be something that feels more urgent. Such is the frenetic life of the teacher.[5]

---

[5]What if you're part-time? It's the same but different. A full-time faculty is hindered from focused evaluation by other responsibilities within the same job. A part-time faculty is hindered from focused evaluation by all their other jobs.

That frantic pace is a blessing and a curse when it comes to self-evaluation. It's a blessing because it is now impossible to stew over every mishap. There are too many mishaps to keep track of and too many other things to do to get hung up on isolated moments. Teachers also—and this is, for me, one of the great blessings of the job—have the opportunity in the very near future to correct whatever just went wrong. During my first full-time teaching semester, I walked out of a Tuesday afternoon New Testament Survey session on Galatians knowing that my students hadn't understood a thing I'd said. In other words, I hadn't taught them. But the next session was only two days later, so on Thursday I walked in and said, "I blew it. That stunk. Let's try Galatians again." No big deal.[6] I stewed for about five minutes Tuesday evening, and then it was time to get back to work.

The quick turnaround is also a curse because it's one thing to realize I blew it and come back the next day or next week to repair the damage. It's another thing to do a deep analysis of a class session and make note of how, next semester or next year, I'll do things differently. Carving out space and time to do that is hard when there are so many more urgent things on

---

[6]No big deal, but actually it is a big deal. A big deal because we all are hindered, by pride, from admitting our failures. A big deal because admitting failure, if done poorly, can destroy your ability to lead (if you're constantly telling them how inexperienced or lousy you are, if you never hold them responsible for anything, if you say, "I'm wrong," but are clearly fishing for someone to say, "No, no, you weren't wrong!"). A big deal because admitting failure, if done well, can give you all kinds of relational equity and position you to lead them far better than you could have if you never owned up to anything being your fault. In this particular case there were quite a few laughs when a student said, "Let me make sure I understand this. You're saying you did a lousy job on Tuesday and didn't really teach us anything?" Yes, that is exactly what I was saying. I had solid rapport with the class as a whole and with that student in particular, so it turned into a constructive moment in more ways than one.

your plate. But if you don't, you're going to make the same mistake next time. And the next time. And the next time. I'm going to head into a session thinking, *I know this one didn't go quite right last time, but I can't remember why, so I'll just do what I did then and hope things magically correct themselves.* This is no way to teach.

First principle that is worth incorporating into your system: *write it down*. "I wrote them down in my diary so that I wouldn't have to remember," says Sean Connery in *Indiana Jones and the Last Crusade*. Trust me: you won't remember. By the time you get up tomorrow, you won't remember, never mind by the next time you teach the course. So write it down. You might remember some highs and lows, a few scattered details, but you won't remember the things that really matter for how to improve that session the next time around.

Second principle: *write it down now*. Not later. Not tomorrow. Not when you have some time. Not over the summer break. Now. The session ends, the students depart, and you write it down. If the classroom is empty for the next period of time, don't even leave the room. Stand where you stood, sit where you sat, whatever, but don't let your brain move on to the next thing until you've taken some time to reflect on what just happened and what needs to happen differently the next time. If another class is coming in immediately after yours, go to your office or some private workspace and write it down. If you have another class in ten minutes, take one of those minutes and write down the most fundamental reflections you can think of. Then come back to them after that next class is over and reflect on both sessions. Don't schedule meetings, to the extent that it's up to you, for at least ten or fifteen minutes after a round in the classroom.

Third principle: *write it down consistently*. What I mean is, have a note-taking style that stays consistent so that you know what you meant by certain things. It's the highlighting principle. Remember when you used to simply highlight things in books that you read, only to realize that when you highlight an entire page, none of it sticks and you don't know why you highlighted any of it in the first place? Make notes on your lesson plan about what raised certain questions, what got off track, what elicited blank stares, where a conversation thrived or broke down, what student insight would be worth incorporating next time, what worked or didn't work about a group activity, etc. Sometimes you can take the next step and make notes about how you're going to adjust things the next time; sometimes you only have to identify where the adjustments need to be made and why. But at a minimum, you need to be able to pick up that lesson plan three months later and understand what your notes mean beyond "this was good" and "this was bad."

Fourth principle: *follow up on what you wrote down*. There's a short game and a long game to this. Ever distribute a handout or worksheet that still has the errors you found last year because you forgot to look at last year's printed (and marked) version and edit the document before reprinting it? I have, and it's unnecessary and unprofessional. Let not the sun go down on your typo. Fix it and fix it now. That's the short game.

Most follow-up is more complicated, of course—I can't just sit down for a moment to "fix" a lousy class session. So part of my system needs to be setting larger chunks of time aside to modify that session before it comes around again. That's the long game. Often this is going to happen over the summer break. (I know, I know, you'd rather be writing that next earth-shattering journal article that four people will read.) You need to at least *look* at all of your reflections before the semester begins again, because some of those reflections are not going to simply change a portion of one session but the whole scope of the course (an unmet course objective, a lousy assignment, etc.). I'll also go into the semester knowing where my weakest points are and plan accordingly.

TAKE A SABBATH

August 2008. My wife, Annie, and I have just moved to Pasadena, CA, and I'm sitting in an orientation session at Fuller Seminary. At one point, Dr. John Goldingay stands up to talk about academics at Fuller, and someone asks him a question about balancing work and rest during a busy season or some such thing. His reply has stayed with me for many years: "The only difference between God and us is that God never thinks he's us." God, in other words, never gets things backward: he knows the universe rises and falls at his command, and he never confuses himself with his creatures. We, on the other hand, are constantly tempted to believe that we are the Creator, the sovereign, the one on whom the future of all things depends. *Sicut deus,* anyone?[7] I am not God. I should stand in front of the mirror every morning and repeat these words: "I am not God. The universe does not rise or fall at my command, and it can handle my absence just fine."

Perhaps the single most difficult element of graduate school is that there are no built-in breaks. The semester never really ends, no one ever tells you to punch out and go home.

---

[7] Dietrich Bonhoeffer, *Creation and Fall*, DBWE 3 (Philadelphia: Fortress, 2004), 31.

That dissertation isn't going to write itself. As a graduate student you can go years without ever really taking a sabbath—and by "sabbath" I mean a stretch of time in which mind and body are enjoying what's been done instead of doing it. Even when the dissertation is written, there's a defense, revisions, and publication—and if you're not already in a job during all that, you're certainly pursuing one. So here's the great lesson that you should have learned during graduate school, and, if you didn't, you'd better learn it now: *we have to take a sabbath.*

- *We* have to take a sabbath. "Sleep is for the weak," I once heard a student say. Yes. And you are weak, and I am weak, and all of us are weak. We are not God. So take a sabbath.

- We have to *take* a sabbath. No one is going to *give* you a sabbath. It's fundamental to the profession: no one is going to send you home and make you leave the work behind, and the work is never going to end. Ever. Welcome to the rest of your life. Just today I heard a retired professor say, "Now that I'm retired I can really get things done." So take a sabbath.

- We have to take a *sabbath*. A *sabbath* is different from a *break*. A break is either doing something different, doing something wasteful, or doing nothing at all. Right now, I'm sitting in a coffee shop, earbuds in, laptop open, writing this book. It's summer, so I'm not overwhelmed by lesson planning, meetings, grading, and the like. I'm taking a *break* from the usual tasks that dominate my work life during the semester. This is a break. It's not a sabbath. I'm working. I'm being productive. I'm creating something that (hopefully!) has professional and financial benefit. That's not sabbath.

So what exactly is a sabbath, and how should we take one (and how often)? There are lots of good resources out there, so I'm not going to reinvent the wheel. But to begin with, sabbath is an *active rest*. It is not passivity. It is not laziness. Nowhere in Scripture will you see sabbath described as doing nothing. Rather, it is (1) active avoidance of certain activities and (2) active participation in other activities. And the "certain activities" to be avoided all fall into a single category: good and right activities that participate in God's creation mandate and are part of a person or community's self-sustenance. In other words, work.[8] Work is what I do to pay the bills, what I do to advance my career, what I do to advance the goodness of God's creation in ways that are necessary for me and my family. Work is coming to creation and saying, "You're not done yet."

Notice, though, that the mere absence of work is not the presence of sabbath. Building is work—but tearing down is not sabbath. Imagine a fast where you only ate junk food instead of your normal healthy diet. This is how some of us conceive of sabbath rest. Instead of filling my mind with the good things of Scripture at my work, I'll fill it with nonsense from YouTube or Netflix. That's not sabbath. That's stupid. That's what Scripture calls "sloth."[9] Sabbath, biblically, is the active movement of mind and body toward God alongside his people. Deny your sinful inclination to idolize yourself by not

---

[8]This is why you don't "sabbath" from sin. You take a sabbath from *good* things, not evil ones.

[9]John Koessler says it so well: "Sloth is rest's dysfunctional relative." John Koessler, *The Radical Pursuit of Rest: Escaping the Productivity Trap* (Downers Grove, IL: InterVarsity Press, 2016), 65.

providing for yourself on the Sabbath.[10] Worship the God who in fact does unfailingly provide for you on the Sabbath. Be in community on the Sabbath (you'll nowhere in Scripture find sabbath depicted as a solo act).

So what does this look like in real time, especially for academics? I can't tell you everything, but here are some suggestions:

- Turn off the communication devices. Seriously. It can wait. And if it can't, someone else will take care of it.

- Catch up on sleep.

- Celebrate the completion of a task even though many other unfinished tasks remain.[11]

- Do something physical.[12]

- Do something that has no direct impact on your career.[13]

- Don't read any books, or, if you do, read books that have absolutely no connection to your field, and don't take any notes on them as you do so.

- Be with people who aren't academics.

---

[10]Leviticus 16:29 says to "deny yourselves and not do any work." You might think that this comes naturally for many of us! But again, it is not laziness—it is the active spiritual discipline of rejecting our natural desire to be self-sustaining.

[11]There are always unfinished tasks. That's not just academia. That's the reality of human existence.

[12]I mention this one because academic work is not "physical" in the blue-collar sense of the word. We definitely burn calories while teaching! But we also sit at our desks and exercise our minds instead of our bodies most of the time. I've discovered through various kinds of work that what is most restful is on the opposite end of the spectrum from my work—when I was a construction worker, sitting on the couch reading was restful. Now that I'm an academic, "rest" most likely means "physical activity that doesn't ask much from my brain."

[13]Deuteronomy 5:15: "Remember that you were slaves in Egypt and that the LORD your God brought you out of there with a mighty hand and an outstretched arm. Therefore the LORD your God has commanded you to observe the Sabbath day." Sabbath-keeping is a declaration of freedom. Slaves don't get a sabbath. You are not a slave to your profession. So take a sabbath.

- Be with people whose presence is restorative.

- Focus your attention on the Creator rather than the creation.

- Enjoy things rather than trying to fix them or analyze them (artistic expressions, for example).

- Find a sabbath rhythm both within and beyond the academic term.[14]

The classroom is overwhelming, especially in the early years. There's no way around that. You're not going to sleep as much as you'd like, you're not going to exercise as much as you'd like, you're not going to have as much time with your family as you'd like. But there's a fine line between admitting up front that it's going to be hard and letting it rule (and ruin) your life. Sabbath is the cornerstone of a teaching life that resists the urge to always work more, do more, produce more; resists the urge to fear failure in the classroom so much that you fail outside the classroom; resists the urge to live the futile life of the person who thinks they are God. So take a sabbath.

CONCLUSION

That last point is an appropriate way to finish: you're not God, so take a sabbath. The early years of teaching are a grind. I mentioned earlier my incredible first full-time gig: 3/3 teaching load, two preps total, lots of mentors, and it was at the institution from which I'd just completed my doctorate, so we didn't have to move. I knew where things were on campus, I had lots

---

[14]A startling command: "Even during the plowing season and harvest you must rest" (Exodus 34:21). Sabbath isn't just for summer break. Even during the busiest seasons (if you've been in agriculture, you understand the implications of this text), take a sabbath.

of friends there, etc. I couldn't have asked for a better start. And it was *insane*. I slept less that year than I had during graduate school. I felt more ineptitude, more fear, and more insecurity than I had at any point while writing my dissertation. And as I learned more fully what needed to be done in order to be a successful teacher, I was as overwhelmed by the enormity of the task as empowered by my knowledge of how to do it. It's *hard*. So at the end of a long list of things to do, on top of everything else you have to do, I'm grateful to wrap the whole thing up by reminding you that you are not God, that neither the universe as a whole nor your classroom in particular stands or falls merely on your efforts.

PART TWO

WHAT TEACHERS MUST KNOW

It might strike you as odd that "doing" comes before "knowing" in this book. This is quite frustrating for the perfectionists among us, who want to know in advance exactly what should happen and what we might do in order to bring it about. In teaching, we never know what we're going to do until after we do it (and then we make a note for next time to do, or not to do, what we just did). We do not know in advance what is going to happen in class today, and the only way to prepare for it is to endure it and then, having done so, to consider what we might do differently if it should happen again. We do not yet know what elements of the class we should determine in advance and which we should not; we do not know how any given student will respond to a particular prompt or reading or lecture. We cannot predetermine whether a particular set of material is best communicated through a lecture or a discussion or a reading or a project; we simply have to try one and see what happens. So now, *after* doing the things that a teacher must do, we now step back and begin to discover the things that a teacher must know.

4

MISSION AND METHOD

Mission and method—where you're trying to go, and how you're planning on getting there. Let's start by going back to the Sierpinski triangle. If I don't know what the top point on the triangle is, I can't orient everything else toward it. I need a mission, and the mission has to be (1) broad enough to direct *every* pedagogical move I make, and (2) specific enough to direct every pedagogical move *I* make. And again, it's not a mistake that we're talking about this after we've done a whole bunch of teaching. We can't know what our mission is without trial and error—until we've taught. From the crucible of practice, the gold of theory emerges. So, for what it's worth, here's my pedagogical mission statement: *That my students would passionately deepen the mystery of God that is expressed in Scripture, by asking Scripture the kinds of questions that lead to fellowship with the triune God and to ever-increasing likeness to Jesus Christ.* It's a work in progress. Six years into this gig, and this is what I have so far. It's probably still too broad, but here's the reasoning behind it.

First, *passion*. I want my students to want something. Not to have already gotten it. Not even to know how to get it, as important as that is. I want them to *want* it. Why? Because fundamentally, we act on our desires. I do what I want to do most. Our desires are regularly in conflict, of course—in such cases we act on our strongest desires. I want to instill in them a strong desire, a hunger-and-thirst level of desire, to know God.

Second, that desire should be to *deepen the mystery*.[1] Because God is unsolvable and incomprehensible, my ultimate pedagogical outcome is one of journey (grow in appreciation of the unending vastness of God) rather than of destination (figure out God—or some similarly absurd thing).

Third, my personal and professional passion is for the study of *Scripture*. I'm not denying the importance of general revelation and the primacy of the incarnation and Pentecost as revelatory acts! But pedagogically speaking, I live and breathe and teach the Bible.

Fourth, the ultimate interpretive skill at the heart of my Hermeneutics courses (and therefore of all my courses) is learning to *ask the right kinds of questions*. This is primarily informed by the Gospel of Mark, in which the disciples' inability to grasp Jesus' message is largely correlated to their typical refusal to admit ignorance. In other words, only when the disciples are willing to admit that they don't understand what's going on, do they ask the kinds of questions that lead to deeper understanding.[2]

---

[1]Thomas Weinandy, borrowing from Gabriel Marcel, speaks of God as a mystery to be discerned rather than a problem to be solved. Thomas G. Weinandy, *Does God Suffer?* (Notre Dame: University of Notre Dame Press, 2000), 30-33.

[2]For positive examples, see Mark 4:10 and 13:3; for the explicit counterpoint, see 9:32. Research upon research demonstrates how difficult this is to achieve. Students,

Fifth, our pedagogical mission ought never to lose sight of the broadest mission of all—the phase where the fractal ends and there is no more zooming out, no more fundamental point toward which the current view is oriented. Fellowship with the triune God. "You have made us and drawn us to yourself, and our heart is unquiet until it rests in you."[3] If my mission isn't part of that mission, it's the wrong mission.

The sixth and final point is a (theologically) obvious corollary to the previous one: ever-increasing likeness to Christ is the byproduct of union with Christ, and union with Christ both is and leads to deeper fellowship with the triune God. But this point isn't here just to keep the theologians happy. The more academic credentials I earn, the more qualified in my field I become, the greater the accomplishments of my students and accolades of my colleagues, the more convinced I am of this—it's all rubbish and emptiness and foolishness alongside actually becoming like Jesus. My job as a professor is to send students out into the church and into the world, and in both places there are a thousand diseased ideas about what it means to be successful. Conformity to the victorious cross of Christ is the antidote to all of them.

So that's my mission. That's where I want to go. But how am I going to get there? The greatest idea in the world is useless unless there's an executable plan in place for accomplishing it.

---

like the disciples, insist on fitting new information into preexisting molds—that is to say, they don't experience "expectation failure," which is what you experience when existing models simply cannot account for the reality in front of you. For the disciples, it takes the cross itself to achieve this. On the pedagogical nuances of this point see especially Ken Bain, *What the Best College Teachers Do* (Cambridge, MA: Harvard University Press, 2004), 27-30.

[3]Saint Augustine, *The Confessions*, trans. Maria Boulding, Vintage Spiritual Classics (New York: Vintage Books, 1997), 1.1.

"Method," in this context, is how we make learning happen in the classroom. Think of it as four interwoven threads: mechanism, mannerism, environment, and centerpiece. *Mechanism*: our delivery (lecture, discussion, group project, quiz). *Mannerism*: our appearance (intense, casual, comic, sloppy, professional). *Environment*: our surroundings (lectern, rows of chairs, arranged tables, socially distanced desks, switch it up every time, coffee shop). *Centerpiece*: our focus (teacher, student, something else).

Mechanism. The mechanism is how the information/value/skill/object/desire/habit is conveyed to our students. Three things are worth noting about our pedagogical mechanism. First, the how is always governed by the why. If your mission in a given course or a given session is to invite students into a story, you might have to do some storytelling. If your mission is to develop in them a certain skill, your how had better include opportunities to practice that skill. My mission centers around them asking certain kinds of questions. Not just certain questions. Certain *kinds* of questions. I can't lecture that, at least not very often. Most of the time, I'm going to put something (a quote, a biblical text, an argument) in front of my students that prompts the right kinds of questions, lead them to actually raise those questions, and go from there. I'm not antilecture! It's just that lecturing is only rarely going to accomplish *my* mission.[4]

---

[4]Reports of the death of the lecture have been greatly exaggerated. TED talks have over sixteen million *subscribers* on YouTube. The top ten videos alone total over two hundred and forty million views. So if you think people just aren't interested in sitting still while someone else does all the talking, think again. If there's a problem with lectures, it isn't that. It is, rather, that too many lectures are long, boring, and focused on content delivery as an end in itself. TED talks are short, compelling, and focused on making an argument whose implications will be spelled out in subsequent conversations.

Second, we should never limit ourselves to only one mechanism even within a single setting. Parenting 101: If I simply *tell* my daughter to do something, it doesn't really matter if I tell her once or ten times—it won't get done. But if I tell her, then show her, then practice with her, then tell her again using different words, then show her again from a different angle, then practice some more . . . okay, it still might not get done. But you get the point. It's naive to think our students can be confronted with a new idea or truth from one angle and just *get it*. No one learns that way. Assign a reading that makes the point from one direction. Then give a minilecture that makes the same point from a different direction. Then have some discussion that reinforces it. Then assign a group project that demonstrates mastery of it.

Third, we need to get better at *all* the mechanisms. We're going to lecture whether we prefer that or not. We're going to lead discussions whether we despise them or not. If you haven't already had this experience, you will, in the years to come, have speaking engagements of more kinds than you thought possible: academic public lectures, class sessions of four, class sessions of forty, weddings, sermons (no mic, handheld mic, lapel mic, over-ear mic—trust me, it makes a difference!), seminars with two hundred, Sunday schools with seven or eight, Q and A sessions, panel discussions, Zoom conferences, premarital counseling sessions, last-minute invitations of various kinds. *We have to keep improving at ALL of these.* It is essential to professional success that we become competent speakers in every imaginable setting.

Mannerism. This is your appearance, your demeanor, your self-presentation. As with everything else, the proper mannerism is at the intersection of your mission and yourself. Despite my location in the ultrarelaxed inland Northwest, the hipster-in-the-coffee-shop vibe doesn't work for me. I'm too intense. Too stiff, maybe. "Too ponderous a person to clown," as Forester put it. That doesn't mean I never step on campus without a suit and tie, or that I don't have a sense of humor, or that I am rude to my students. But in my context, informality is next to godliness, and that's sometimes a problem.[5] A degree of formality is required if you want to take something seriously, and I want my students to take encounters with the triune God in his Word very seriously. And lest this sound prescriptive, as though every Bible or theology faculty should do likewise, let me be clear: my mannerism is toward the formal end of the spectrum because it fits me *and* it fits my mission. Another person with basically the same mission could accomplish it through a different mannerism because that other person is not me.

Mark Jonas, professor of education at Wheaton College, calls this your *persona*. It's not a mask to hide the real you; quite the opposite, in fact. It's taking *off* the mask that you wear the rest of the time. It's an extreme version of you, the exaggerated you. It's acting out the most (appropriately) honest version of yourself. Are you a nerd? Be *more* nerdy in the classroom. Are you a sports nut? Talk about sports *incessantly* in the classroom. Are you a pun master? This will come naturally to you because you don't know how to quit anyway. But Jonas warns that your persona must first of all be *for the benefit of your students*. I'm amping up myself in the classroom for their sake. It's uncomfortable to be

---

[5]We recently received a report from some of the local businesses with which our students had been interning that was positive in nearly every respect *except professional appearance*. If my students gaining employment after graduation is an institutional value, it is part of my responsibility to train them toward that end.

the real me, but I'm not doing it for me. I'm doing it for them. And they need to know that. Jonas also warns that your persona should draw attention to the material, not to you. It's not that hard to tell the difference between a fan that's going crazy because they love the team and a fan that's going crazy in order to get attention for themselves. Your nerdiness, your sports fanaticism, your formality or informality, your intensity, whatever it is, should be fully on display not for its own sake (you don't talk about sports just because you like sports), not for reputation's sake (you don't talk about sports so you can become known as the prof who is obsessed with sports), but for the sake of learning.

Environment. Environment is underappreciated simply because we don't realize that there are options. It's one of the few ways in which tremendous flexibility in the carrel somehow becomes a complete lack thereof in the classroom. Straight or arced rows of chairs or tables, lectern at the front. Maybe a rectangular arrangement of tables or circle of chairs if there are less than ten students. Why? Because that's the way we've always done it.

Look at the room and think about your students. Arrangement of persons is one thing. Lighting is another. Ambience. Decor. Access. Line of sight. How comfortable do you want them to be? If others in the room will be speaking, does it matter if anyone can hear them and see them? Do you want them to be speaking to you only or to the others as well? What kind of surface do they need in order to do what you need them to do? Will they be shifting chairs or desks or tables around midsession for one activity or another? For the online teachers out there: How's the lighting? Are there background noises? What's on the wall behind you that might distract your students the entire session? If they can't see you and can't hear you, it's hard to call it teaching. Have you communicated with your students about their needs with respect to light and sound and technical requirements?

Now look at the room and think about *you*. Think about comfort and think about effectiveness. Comfort—you need to control the environment so that you aren't distracted by tripping over cords, fiddling with the microphone, failing to hear the quiet person in the back row, leaning awkwardly on the lectern (this one is a problem for me!), constantly dropping and picking up notes, clickers, and markers (ditto). How are your notes and computer and texts and clicker and markers (or whatever other items you use) arranged so you aren't constantly losing them? Effectiveness—how can you best communicate at any given moment? Do you need to sit down with them at the table so that you can maintain a sense of closeness and community, and so that you can get up and get excited at the appropriate time? Or do you prefer to sit and pound the table when you want to make *that* point? Do you need to carry everything in your hand so that you can most easily march up and down the aisle, or back and forth across the stage? Do you need more whiteboards? (I *always* need more whiteboards. One of these summers I'm going to buy a ton of whiteboard paint and hit every classroom wall on campus.) And again to those teaching from digital platforms: Are you comfortably seated? Do you have reliable internet? Is your headset or speaker system audible to the rest of the "room"? Do you have adequate space to put physical materials (or digital materials via a second monitor, perhaps) on the desk in front of you?

Centerpiece. I'll be honest: I think there's only one right answer to this one. And if you don't agree, Parker Palmer wants to talk to you: "The classroom should be neither teacher-centered nor student-centered but subject-centered. . . . This is a classroom in which student and teacher alike are focused on a great thing."[6]

First question: What is that one great thing? In my classes, it's the Scriptures. Not information about the Scriptures. Not one particular interpretation—or the range of interpretations —of the Scriptures. The biblical text itself is the "great thing" toward which my gaze, being no different than my students' gaze, is directed. The great thing in your classroom might be a certain body of literature. It might be an artifact or set of artifacts. It might be a language or a culture or a people. It's whatever makes the class worth having in the first place.

Second question: How do we teach such that neither we nor our students are the ultimate goods of the classroom? It starts by bringing what we loved most about research into teaching. I don't mean the silence or the isolation. I mean the thing itself. We didn't go to graduate school for fame or fortune. (If you did, I trust you have since been enlightened.) We went because there was this *thing*, this subject, this question, that took hold of us. We endured because we loved that great thing on the desk in front of us. We read mind-numbingly tedious scholarly essays because there was some chance they might bring us closer to that great thing. We learned new languages. We passed comprehensive exams. We wrote theses. We accepted intense criticism. We slept little, earned little, worked much, spent

---

[6]Parker Palmer, *The Courage to Teach: Exploring the Inner Landscape of a Teacher's Life*, 10th Anniversary ed. (San Francisco: John Wiley & Sons, 2007), 119.

much. We didn't do this just for fun. We didn't do it just because we wanted to teach. We did it because we found outside of ourselves a great thing around which to center not just our research but our whole existence. And to be clear, I don't mean the dissertation itself. No dissertation is as important as all that. I mean the subject matter, the fertile ground out of which the dissertation grew. Put *that* at center stage in the classroom.

Concretely, then, how does this happen? First, direct their gaze toward the thing rather than toward you. When a question is posed and they look at you (as they invariably will), direct them back to the thing. We cannot answer all the questions for them, or they will seek answers from us rather than from it. Second, do not accept all answers as valid or they will seek the answers in themselves alone, which is at least as bad as seeking them in us. Do not be afraid to correct them on the basis of the one great thing in the middle of the room, and do not be afraid to permit them to correct you in similar fashion. Third, do not make yourself the hero of every story. Tell them of your failures as much as, if not more than, your successes. Fourth, choose their secondary teachers wisely. I mean the books and essays and videos and podcasts and research sources toward which we send them. If those sources don't point the students toward that one great thing, we need to find other sources that do.

5

COMMUNITY

It's a classic John Grisham courtroom scene. Mordecai Green, representing the family of the recently deceased Lontae Burton against the corporation that evicted her and sent her and her four children to their deaths in the snowy streets of Washington, DC, is told what the going rate is for unemployed single mothers and their children in wrongful death suits. But Green

> didn't care what juries were doing in Dallas or Seattle, and failed to see the relevance. He had no interest in judicial proceedings in Omaha. He knew what he could do with a jury in the District, and that was all that mattered. . . . "You got a wealthy lawyer from a wealthy firm deliberately allowing a wrongful eviction to occur, and as a direct result my clients got tossed into the streets where they died trying to stay warm. Frankly, gentlemen, it's a beautiful punitive damages case, especially here in the District."[1]

---

[1]John Grisham, *The Street Lawyer* (New York: Bantam Doubleday Dell, 1998), 306.

KNOW YOUR STUDENTS

We are awash today in data. We can learn a great deal about our students—before they set foot in our classrooms—through nationwide trends, institutional surveys, and other means. We can keep track of what it means that the next incoming class will now be more Gen Z than millennial. We can know how many of them are on prescription medication (most of them), their economic and racial profiles, their reasons for coming to our institutions, and on and on the list goes. There's certainly nothing wrong with accessing this information. But knowing about our students collectively and theoretically will never be a replacement for knowing them individually and concretely. Forget the trends, says Green—what matters is what's happening right here, right now. We ought not think that we understand our students simply because we have read the latest research about the collective that they may or may not represent. We need to know them, not theories about them.

First principle: *know their names.* This isn't rocket science. Get a picture roster of your class from the registrar's office before day one. Memorize the names and the faces the best you can—that student who has dyed their hair over the break is going to be tough, but when you get them wrong on the first try they'll probably say, "Oh, I dyed my hair over the break so I don't look anything like my picture." You'll both laugh, and they'll appreciate that you tried and that you have a sense of humor about the whole thing. Start early—get the roster a week or so in advance and commit the names to memory. Got a hundred students across four courses this semester? Start earlier. Any student you can't name by the third session has effectively dropped the class.

Second principle: *eat where they eat, and live where they live.*
The particulars of any given school pose all sorts of challenges
to this principle. Some institutions reside in neighborhoods
well beyond the financial reach of its employees. Some institutions are so residential-life dominant that students rarely leave
campus. Some are predominantly commuter campuses attended by individuals who are part-time student, full-time
worker. In such cases as these, we still have options. Frequent
the same coffee shops as our students. Eat lunch either in the
cafeteria or in public, on-campus spaces where you can interact
with them. Be present, as is reasonably possible, at campus
events.[2] And if all else fails, invite them into your homes. What
college student doesn't jump at the chance to get a legit home-
cooked meal and some time away from campus once in a while?

Third principle: *ask questions and write down the answers later.*
I interact with far too many people in general, and students in
particular, to remember what they tell me. So after class, or after
a meeting (not during the meeting—I'm not interviewing
them!), I take a moment to write down the key points of the
conversation. Some of it is basic biography (where they are
from, what they are studying, potential career paths) and some
of it is more personal (struggles they are currently undergoing,
significant moments at college, fundamental realities of their
life, specific things I learned from their behavior during class).

---

[2]Especially at a larger institution, pick a single kind of event and be a consistent presence there. If you enjoy the football games, go to all the football games—or concerts
or academic lectures or art shows or whatever. Pick a space in which at least some of
your students will appear, *and that fits you,* and appear regularly in it. Don't try to be
everywhere always—you are trying to make yourself available to your students and
get to know them, not to become one of them. Don't, Gary Burge admonishes us,
fall into the "poser" trap: imagining that "if I am just one of them, I'll be liked."
Gary M. Burge, *Mapping Your Academic Career: Charting the Course of a Professor's
Life* (Downers Grove, IL: IVP Academic, 2015), 39.

I have a 3×5 card for each person, and—in case it needs to be said—these cards are for my eyes only. No exceptions. And when I prepare to go back into the classroom with them or meet again with them, our interactions are far more likely to be meaningful, instead of the "Tell me about yourself. . . . I know you've mentioned this in the past, but remind me . . . where are you from again?" conversations that I'll end up having otherwise.

Fourth principle: *pursue them*. Don't get weird. Don't be inappropriate. If you're not sure where some of those boundaries are, ask your mentor, your dean, your spouse.[3] But you are trying to *teach* them, and if they're not getting taught, you're not teaching.[4] And if they're not getting taught, there's a reason why. It might be because you just aren't communicating very well in class. But if thirty out of thirty-four students are getting it, and four aren't, the problem likely goes beyond in-class pedagogy. So we need to pursue those four and figure out what's going on. It might be a back-home situation. It might be that they're overcommitted and drowning in responsibilities. It might be that we simply haven't connected with them personally, so they're not connecting with us personally either. It might be that we said something three weeks ago that rubbed them the wrong way. There are a million variables here, and it's *extremely* unlikely that a student is going to initiate the necessary conversation. We have to pursue them.

Fifth principle: *invite them into challenging situations*. These might be in class or they might be extracurricular. They might be conversation-based (any conversation about biblical gender

---

[3]See Burge, *Mapping Your Academic Career*, 54-55.
[4]The most important points are also the simplest. If they're not learning, you're not teaching. See Bruce Wilkinson, *The Seven Laws of the Learner* (Sisters, OR: Multnomah, 1992), 23-31.

roles is sure to generate discussion) and they might be event-based (study abroad programs, anyone?). Lots of options here. The goal is to make them safely uncomfortable—meaning, they trust us enough to go with us into new spaces, even if those spaces are going to push some buttons and raise some questions and stretch them a little (or a lot).

Sixth principle (forgive me if I am a bit long-winded on this one!): *set reasonable expectations for them.* In his classic book *A Little Exercise for Young Theologians,* Helmut Thielicke takes aim at the tendency of beginning theology students to grow much faster intellectually than spiritually.[5] This isn't surprising, really. Spend ten or twenty or thirty hours per week studying the Bible, and you're going to learn a lot about it—a lot more, in fact, than you could possibly put into practice in that amount of time.[6] This developmental mismatch is not necessarily a bad thing. What is a bad thing is our tendency to equate intellectual growth with spiritual growth, as though learning a lot of stuff in college or seminary were the same thing as maturation toward Christ. As though someone were equipped to teach or preach or pastor or otherwise lead in the church simply by

---

[5]Helmut Thielicke, *A Little Exercise for Young Theologians,* trans. Charles L. Taylor (Grand Rapids, MI: Eerdmans, 1962), 28.

[6]I'm talking about our students, but let's not kid ourselves—if a bachelor's degree in theology inevitably causes a developmental gap, how much more so a master's degree or a doctorate? Has our personal growth kept up with our intellectual advancement? Whether your field is literature or physics or theology or communication, your professional knowledge has real-life implications. Have you ascended the heights to which your intellectual heroes have summoned you? Not likely. I teach on the doctrine of the Trinity. Does my life reflect in full the implications of that doctrine? I devote a portion of one course to work, rest, and laziness. Suffice it to say I have not yet arrived at the destination toward which my teaching points! Again, this is inevitable. I don't live up to the standards of my own knowledge, and I never will, partly because feeding my brain is what I do for a living. But knowing this should inspire me to (1) strive toward that which I will never fully attain, and (2) always be willing to admit my mistakes.

virtue of possessing a theology degree or two. There's a reason such things as entry-level jobs exist even in environments where a college degree is a prerequisite. We all know that studying to know is not the same as being prepared to do, whether in theology or any other arena.

Of what import is this for the professor? Much in every way! First, we need to recognize this disproportionate growth in our students when we speak with them or about them. The most brilliant student is going to make the most absurd mistakes, the academic overachiever is going to experience the greatest personal failure. Professional success beyond the classroom is not straightforwardly foreshadowed by excellence in the classroom. We know all this, but we are still snared by the false belief that success in our academic ecosystem guarantees success in the ecosystem to come.

Second, we need to encourage students to grow beyond the classroom and to be patient about that growth. You can cram knowledge; you cannot expedite wisdom. How often the recent college graduate feels that he or she is ready to go out and change the world, only to find that the world does not want to change and no amount of textbook recitation will overcome that stubbornness! College marketers, take note: College does not prepare you to change the world. Stop telling prospective students otherwise.[7] Curriculum revision committees, take note: College does not prepare you to change the world. Stop trying to design programs that do. More classes, fewer classes, different classes, new objectives or programs or systems or

---

[7]It is of little wonder that so many people in the United States today think college is a waste of time and money. If the product doesn't do what the product says it will do, we stop buying the product.

whatever—endless tinkering will not change the fact that only so much can be accomplished in three or four years. I am certainly not suggesting that those years are solely about knowledge and that wisdom can wait until after you graduate. There is a way to offer knowledge that pertains to wisdom and values wisdom and encourages the development of wisdom. But the kind of wisdom it takes to move the world in a new direction is unlikely to develop within the structures of an undergraduate degree, and that's okay. This means two things: that we admit a bachelor's degree is a beginning rather than an end and that we encourage students to live beyond the classroom even while the bulk of their waking moments are devoted to the classroom.

KNOW YOUR FAMILY

This one might be a surprise—when we think about our academic community, we naturally think about students, colleagues, staff, and administration. Fair enough. I've said a few things already about knowing your students, and there are lots of other resources out there to help you navigate getting to know your coworkers. But I want to say a bit about your family, because, well, in case you hadn't noticed, the academic career is hard on families. Finances. Schedule. Stress. Instability. Insecurity. And if you haven't discovered this already, you will soon—none of these magically disappear just because you get a full-time job, if you get a full-time job. Maybe these things fade eventually. Maybe my situation is unique. Maybe everyone else has figured this stuff out already. I certainly haven't, so I'm speaking to those of you who are like me—those who are weighed down not only by the pressures of academic life but by the effect those pressures have on your families. And the most

I can do at this stage is share what I've learned (usually the hard way) at this stage.

Communication. I have to communicate with Annie about what I need to do and why I need to do it, and we need to be partners in the decision-making process. At this point in my career, I rarely say yes to anything beyond my basic job requirements (teaching and administration) before processing it with her. An opportunity to speak at a church or high school or conference of some sort. An invitation to meet with students outside normal working hours. Anything that's going to change our normal routine is going to be a joint decision. And after working on this for a decade or so, some things have become clear about those joint decisions.

First, her instincts are usually right. If she anticipates a new commitment being a problem, we're probably going to say no. Second, I know her limits and she knows mine. We know at this point that I get sick when I'm working too much, that she gets overwhelmed when she feels like she's single-parenting, that I need to exercise regularly, that she needs seven and a half to eight hours of sleep every night. The math isn't always that hard: if these things are going to go wrong on account of accepting a new responsibility, the answer is no. Third, when we make a decision together, we bear the consequences together. We've made some poor calls, in hindsight. When *I* make those calls, conflict happens. But when *we* make those calls, healthy processing and a stronger marriage happens. We're going to be wrong sometimes, but we're going to be wrong together.

Partnership. Annie and I work together. We have what looks like a pretty traditional family setup: I work primarily outside the home, she works primarily inside the home, homeschools our kids, etc. But from the beginning of our marriage we've wanted to work together, and that happens in two ways: at home and at school. At home, there are a few things only Annie can do and a few things only I can do. Everything in between is fair game, and we are forever tweaking our systems and expectations. Working together at home also means it's rare that one of us is working while the other isn't, unless sleep is involved (I can get by on less sleep than Annie, so I usually do the early shift with the kids, but it wasn't that long ago that I would keep sleeping while she fed an infant). I'm not watching the game while she's putting the kids down, she isn't reading a magazine while I'm making dinner—unless we've specifically planned to do things that way in advance. This might be more about our stage of life (small children) than anything else, but between 6:00 a.m. and 8:00 p.m. there's hardly a moment where work isn't being done by someone. And for us, if one of us is working, the other is as well.[8]

At school it's a bit different, obviously. I spend a lot more time at home than Annie does at my workplace. But as we are partners at home, we are partners in my work. This means, as I mentioned earlier, that any work decision with implications for Annie is going to be discussed with Annie. It also means that we are going to find some way for Annie to be part of what's going on at Great Northern University.

As I write this, I am sitting on my bed while my wife, Annie, is downstairs leading a prayer group attended by several of my female students. I greet them at the door, chat for a couple of minutes while we get dessert, and then I disappear for two or

---

[8]Because it needs to be said: Dads out there, we do not babysit our kids. We parent them. This is part of what it means to partner with our spouses.

three hours while they talk and laugh and cry and pray together. It's one of the highlights of my professional life, strange though that may sound, because Annie gets to be a part of it. We have three small children right now, so her daytime availability is limited (to put it mildly). But every other Thursday night, we are colaborers for the mission of Great Northern University.

In my previous job, Annie was a bit more removed from campus life, and that turned out to be a tremendous blessing. Two years of continuous drama climaxed in a sudden campus-closure announcement, and Annie's separation from that drama enabled her to be a stabilizing presence in my chaos. I came home every day churning and stressed and confused and angry and all the rest, and the fact that Annie wasn't mixed up in the situation meant she could handle my decompression and verbal processing. So in that season, our working "together" mostly meant Annie looking at the situation objectively and being a sounding board for my frustration. But I want to name that season as an aberration, not a norm, and we both prefer our current reality wherein she is actively involved in my work even if in a necessarily limited fashion.

Awareness. My vocation is hard on my family. I need to be aware of this all the time. I need to be aware that my family carries a portion of my professional insecurity from GRE to 401(k). That annual academic conferences are the highlight of my professional year, but my stay-at-home-with-the-kids spouse has a different perspective. That a two-hour conversation with a student can really hurt Annie when she's gone a week without thirty consecutive minutes of my undivided attention (the situation that brought about such a long engagement with the student, however serious, isn't really the point). That voicing my fears with respect to professional success or job security (which is, obviously, sometimes appropriate and necessary) at the wrong time or in the wrong way can be a serious trigger for Annie, and we end up tearing each other down precisely when we needed to be built up.

Please note: I'm not saying you shouldn't go to conferences. I'm not saying you shouldn't ever relocate to improve your professional situation. I'm not saying you shouldn't, on certain occasions, spend a significant amount of time with a student or coworker. And you know from my testimony above that I'm not saying you should never bring work drama home. What I am saying is that these situations have fantastic potential for tearing your family apart if you are not aware of how your family is affected by them. Take yearly travel, for example. Recognizing that five or six days away every November for conferences is really hard on Annie helps her partner with me in those trips—it helps more, I should note, than telling her how important these trips are, or reporting on all the professional benefits once I get home. And planning in advance a night or a weekend away for her when I return helps even more! Communicating awareness is good; acting on it is better.

Navigating the work-family dynamic as an academic is hard. Hard because most of us are lousy at turning it off when we come home. Hard because graduate school taught us that there's no such thing as a vacation until you're *done*. Hard because so little of our schedule is externally imposed. Hard because it takes a long time, if it happens at all, for our chosen vocation to pay more than it cost (financially, that is). I make mistakes in this department all the time. But I try to be quick to apologize, Annie tries to be quick to forgive, and we both try to be quick to avoid making the same mistakes again and again. And as long we keep communicating, as long as we see each other as partners rather than opponents, and as long as I stay clued in to how my professional world affects her and the kids, we're going to be alright.

6

LIMITATIONS

This is partly about sabbath, obviously. You have the usual set of creaturely limitations, and ignoring them will lead to burnout and failure. But you have other limitations, too, though these aren't going to be about what you *can't* do as much as what you probably *shouldn't* do. These limitations are particular to you—your family situation, your institution, your financial realities, your life circumstances. These are situations in which you simply say, "It's not in the cards for me to take that on."

The principle here is quite simple: you can't do everything, and everything you choose to do is a choice not to do something else. Every time you say yes to one thing, you say no to everything else. I am sitting at my desk writing this book, which means I am not doing anything else. I am not grading. I am not fulfilling committee responsibilities. I am not researching. I am not spending time with my family. I am not exercising. Multitasking is a myth. I can only do one thing at a time. Every second is filled with one thing and not another. My limitations, therefore, are largely self-imposed. I chose this morning to limit my sleep so that I could get some exercise. I chose to limit my social media time because I value talking to my children more than I value looking at pictures of your children. I chose to chat with a coworker on the way down the hall to my office, which means, necessarily, that I chose not to use those ten minutes to write emails or work on this book or get any other task done. *I can't opt out of limitations.* I can choose how I limit myself; I cannot choose whether or not to have limits.

Awareness of the self-imposed nature of our limitations is especially important given the kind of flexibility we enjoy in the academic vocations. Outside of meetings and class time, when was the last time anyone required you to work on a particular task right now (and even with meetings and class time, you have varying degrees of ownership over the when, the where, and the what)? As long as the job gets done, no one really cares when you do it—and you've heard enough stories about publishing "deadlines" to know that even the when is mostly up to you (to the chagrin of publishers, obviously—I'm not recommending that you push your luck in that department!). By and large, you decide, moment by moment, how to use (limit) your time.

So the question is less, How much can you accomplish? and more, What, exactly, do you want to accomplish? And the follow-up is always, What am I opting *out* of accomplishing when I opt *into* accomplishing what I want to accomplish? On the one hand, there's always fat to be trimmed—most of it, for most of us, is technology related. Every time you look at your phone, you opt out of getting anything done. Every time I check my Facebook feed, I opt out of accomplishing anything else. On the other hand, you have to consciously choose among

professional and personal goods. If I simply say yes to everything that comes my way, I am going to end up saying no to
(1) doing any of those things particularly well, (2) all valuable
nonwork related activities (family, exercise, sleep), or (3) my
ability to gauge in any given moment what is most valuable for
me to be doing on any basis other than the most pressing
deadline. Is that price worth paying? Knowing your limitations
is as much about knowing what you *don't* care to get done as it
is what you *do* want to get done.

Obviously, the "right" answers to these questions are going
to vary tremendously from individual to individual. But here
are some general points of wisdom (to the degree that I can
claim wisdom at my career stage!), stemming as much from my
mistakes as from my successes.

Play the long game. Graduate school taught you endurance
within a single project—now work out that endurance over a
lifetime. "A long obedience in the same direction," as Eugene
Peterson put it.[1] Tenure is a blip on the radar. Necessary and
important? Sure. Of equal value to family and physical health?
Not on your life. I've never heard a senior professor wish they
had spent less time with their families. And you can't be a
productive academic if you're constantly in and out of the
hospital—never mind the financial pressures that accompany
frequent health issues.

Stay out of the rat race. There are graduate students, right now,
with enough publications to get tenure. Some of them, to be
frank, alternate between social media posts about their latest
peer-reviewed essay and posts about their latest anxiety-induced

---

[1]Eugene Peterson, *A Long Obedience in the Same Direction: Discipleship in an Instant
Society* (Downers Grove, IL: InterVarsity, 1980).

medical emergency. And speaking of social media—if you have three hundred Facebook friends who are academics, and they average one publication each, per year, you're going to see something published just about every single day on your feed. It's impossible *not* to feel inadequate.

Self-identify. N. T. Wright once characterized his own approach as "blasting away with a shotgun in hope of the occasional hit," contrasted with that of his good friend Richard Hays, who had "paused, pondered, and written masterpieces that have changed the whole discussion."[2] Nothing is necessarily wrong with either approach, but we have to know that we can't publish as much as Wright and be as laser focused as Hays. And sometimes we have to do what needs to be done, regardless of whether we feel particularly gifted for or enthusiastic about that task (grading and administrative work probably comes to mind).[3] But to the degree that it is possible, understand where your strengths and weaknesses are and operate out of your strengths.

The professorial life, particularly for those of us whose work is primarily teaching (as opposed to research or administration), holds a particularly insidious risk as far as knowing our limitations. In the wise words of Chuck Swindoll, "I never learn while talking and I talk too much."[4] I had a stretch, once, that involved a chapel message on Wednesday, a two-day seminar on Thursday and Friday, a wedding on Saturday, and a sermon

---

[2]N. T. Wright, *Paul and the Faithfulness of God*, 2 vols. (Minneapolis: Fortress, 2013), preface.

[3]I am currently part of a university startup, and we are all recruiters, fundraisers, marketers, student life coordinators, administrators, and, of course, teachers. Much of the time, the question is less, What would suit me best? and more, What does the mission require?

[4]Not *technically* true, of course; verbal processing certainly has its place!

on Sunday. Oh, and a full teaching load mostly packed into Monday and Tuesday. I don't know that I've ever been as tired as I was after that week.

I learned many lessons through that brief period of insanity, like, "Don't sign up for so many things back-to-back-to-back," and, "Next time, make sure at least four of those speaking opportunities are on the same topic." But the most important lesson I learned was that *I loved every minute of it*. It was one of the most exhilarating weeks of my life. I loved it. And what I loved most of all was the sound of my own voice. All day, every day, *me*. Me, the one with the loudest voice in the room. Me, the center of attention (well, except for the wedding—but presiding over a wedding is an intoxicating exercise of power even while all eyes are on the bride and groom). I've never done so much talking in a seven-day span, and I had just enough sense about me to realize, at the end, how dangerous that was.

Some years ago, I met with a group of pastors—older men who had been in pastoral ministry for many years. We were sitting around, conversing about . . . well, that's not quite right. We weren't conversing. We were *competing*. Competing for airtime. Competing for everyone else's attention. Competing to be the dominant voice in the room. First, it was frustrating because I was losing the competition. Then it was annoying because someone else was winning the competition. And finally, it was terrifying because I realized the game we were playing—and I didn't want any part of it.

It's always going to be a temptation for those whose vocation involves speaking (and especially spiritual leadership coupled with speaking) to grow used to the sound of one's own voice. Few things foster arrogance like being viewed as an expert. But

on that particular occasion, watching those men fight for pre-
eminence in the room, I think I gained some insight into factors
that can take you from the temptation to the reality. Those men
who seemed to me to be the first among us sinners had a couple
of things in common. First, they had all gained positions of
leadership unseasonably early in their careers. Senior pastors
in their twenties, for example. Second, they had all lacked
mentors during those leadership experiences. I even heard one
of them remark that he had asked God for a mentor, and God's
response had been, "No, you go be a mentor." I'll be blunt: I
don't think that response was from God.

So from my own experience of falling in love with the sound
of my voice, and from witnessing how that love increases over
decades of being the most important person in the room, I'm
learning (read: trying to put into practice) a couple of things.

First, we need to keep some people close who are in our profession but aren't overly impressed with us. Peer review is a wonderful thing, whether in print or in conference settings, because
every one of us can convince our students of things that would
get us laughed out of the room in a professional context. Just
because my students think I'm brilliant doesn't mean I am. Such
praise is more highly prized when coming from other scholars.[5]

Second, we need to keep some people close who *aren't* in our
profession, and therefore aren't overly impressed with us. Some
outsiders are duly impressed, of course—they think it's
amazing that you're a published author, that you went to
graduate school, that you know *so much*. I don't mean those
people. I mean the ones who want to know whether your

---

[5]Of course, some of us gain distinction in this setting as well, leading to what one of
my colleagues calls "the temptation to never have an unpublished thought."

academic knowledge actually matters for "real life." Does it make you a better spouse, help you when the plumbing is backed up, improve the life of anyone around you, pay the bills, or bring you closer to God in a practical way? You can look down your nose at such people, or you can pay attention to them. They might be wrong about the value of the intellectual life, but their blank stares or cynical snorts when you start waxing eloquent are going to keep you in your place.

Third, we need to keep some people close who love us too much, and care too deeply about the community of which we are a part, to let us dominate the room. In that group of pastors there were some who sat back and clearly didn't feel the need to compete. One, in particular, was the host of the event. Like the others, he had become a senior pastor in his twenties. Like the others, he had become the loudest voice in the room much too early. But I think I know at least part of what went differently for him because I've been in his home. It's a loud home. It's a home with a lot of energy and multiple conversations at once and plenty of laughter and excitement. You might think that's the kind of home that fosters competitive conversation styles, because it's so loud that everyone is having to shout above the din. But it wasn't like that. There was a coherence to the noise, like the noise was a team effort, like the energy in the room was precisely the result of *everyone* playing a part, rather than one person doing the whole job themselves. And I laugh just thinking about one person trying to do the whole job, trying to place themselves at the center of the room. The ball just moved too quickly for that. And when the philosophy of the team is to keep the ball moving, you know what happens when one player holds on to it for too long. They get benched, they get avoided, they get ignored. No one wants to play with a ball hog, no matter how gifted (except for James Harden, maybe). Put yourself on a team that doesn't want anyone to hog the ball and is willing to deal with people who do.

Fourth, and finally, we need to cultivate a habit of careful listening. Not listening so you're ready with your next comment. Not listening so you have some ammunition to fire back at them. Actually listening. Who knows, we might learn something! And even if we don't, we'll do the rest of the room a favor by giving them a break from listening to us. One of my dreams for the Great Northern University communications department is that one day we'll have an entire class on *listening*. (No, I won't be teaching it. But I should probably take it.) Can you imagine that? And—shameless plug for my future alumni— how do you think those students are going to do on the job market? Who *doesn't* want to work with people who are excellent listeners? "The wise in heart accept commands, but a chattering fool comes to ruin" (Prov 10:8).

We need to know our limits. And sometimes the limit isn't defined by how much I can get done but by how much I can get done without falling in love with the sound of my own voice. Or to put it in sabbath terms: I am not God, the world is somehow sustained apart from my voice, in fact the world might actually be *better* apart from my voice, and I preach this truth to myself every time I forego an opportunity to speak.

7

POWER

Do you want to be a teacher?[1] James isn't going to mince words: this is not necessarily a good idea. "Not many of us should become teachers, brothers and sisters, because we will be judged more strictly" (Jas 3:1 ESV). Teachers will be judged more strictly because it is our business to shape those around us by speaking. To speak, he tells us, is to run the risk of setting the world on fire, releasing a great evil, injecting everyone within the sound of our voice with a deadly poison (Jas 3:6, 8). And, of course, the risk is in direct proportion to your skill: the best teachers can do the most damage because their words have the most power.[2] So the more effective we become at teaching, the more seriously we should take James's admonition.

---

[1]Some insist on a distinction between a *teacher* and a *professor*, and that's fine. I'm using the term "teacher" here in a more general sense: someone who, among other things, teaches.

[2]More of us than we would care to admit will likely echo Seneca's profound confession: "When I think of all I have said, I envy the dumb." Seneca, *On the Happy Life*, in *Moral Essays, Volume II: De Consolatione ad Marciam. De Vita Beata. De Otio. De Tranquillitate Animi. De Brevitate Vitae. De Consolatione ad Polybium. De Consolatione ad Helviam*, trans. John W. Basore, Loeb Classical Library 254 (Cambridge, MA: Harvard University Press, 1932), 2.3.

This warning does not merely heighten our awareness of how serious our profession is. It also redefines what it means to fail as a teacher. First, eloquence, knowledge, and pedagogical skill are no guarantee of success—all those things can simply make it easier to burn the world down.

Second, failure is in its effects. When I reflect on a "failed" teaching session, I tend to think of circumstances in which my words had little to no effect. My students didn't understand what I said, didn't appreciate what I said, weren't adequately impressed with what I said. But for James, "failure" can also happen when our words have the *wrong* effect. I speak falsely, and my students believe me and therefore believe falsely. I speak arrogantly, and my students are either put off by my arrogance and so miss whatever truth that arrogance masked, or else they take on my arrogance and perpetuate it. Or, to come back to the "no effect" point, there really isn't any such thing as ineffective words. If my words are "ineffective," my students will believe that (1) I'm not worth listening to (which might be true), and (2) the topic on which I am speaking is not worth engaging (which ought not be true). "It is a sin to bore people with the Bible," Howard Hendricks used to say. Perhaps we should expand that claim: it is a sin to bore people with anything that is worth knowing, because in their boredom they are led to believe that the thing itself is boring and useless and unworthy of interest.

Third, failure is about them, not about us. The fact is, my post-session broodings are usually about me. I didn't live up to my expectations. I just didn't get the job done that session. I didn't make the impact that I hoped to make. I wasn't on my game this morning. I've said these things in my head or to a colleague a thousand times. They're all true, but they're all about me.

They're all about my ego. They're all accompanied by fears about student evaluations, enrollment in later semesters, reputation on campus, chances of promotion, and the like. And James would say that if these are the things that drive me as a teacher, I have already failed. It's not about me. It's about my students. Have they learned? Have they taken hold of the "one great thing" (shout-out to Parker Palmer) that stands at the center of my classroom—or, better yet, has that one great thing taken hold of them? True pedagogical evaluation aims at the heart and life of the student, not the reputation or ego of the professor.[3]

Speaking of reputation and ego (how's that for a transition?), it is not only our students who are affected by our teaching. Our reach is far more extensive than that. It's like what King Lemuel's mother said to him: "It is not for kings, Lemuel—it is not for kings to drink wine, not for rulers to crave beer, lest they drink and forget what has been decreed, and deprive all of the oppressed of their rights" (Prov 31:4-5). It sounds like something you may have heard before (forgive yet another reference to the Marvel Cinematic Universe): with great power comes great responsibility. It's sort of the next step, actually: with great responsibility comes the need for great self-control. And since those of us who speak for a living take a great responsibility upon themselves (in light of what James says about burning the world down), well, you can fill in the rest. But as obvious as Lemuel's mom's words might be—that excessive alcohol intake is a bad idea for those who talk for a living—that's not quite the target I've got in my sights. Nope. It's social media.

---

[3]I recently heard Heather Day (associate professor of communication at Colorado Christian University), on the *Theology in the Raw* podcast with Preston Sprinkle, say it this way: "Communication is about the listener, not the speaker" (episode 776).

Roll your eyes if you like. Diatribes on the dangers of social media are as common as the dangers themselves. Many of you already know this and wouldn't dream of doing the things I'm going to speak out against. And yet, if my Facebook feed is any judge, there are plenty of academics (especially early-career academics, perhaps) who haven't taken those diatribes to heart. So here comes one more rant—well, I hope it's not a rant. I hope it's a good long look at my own heart. The finger points there first.

Issue #1: Slander. The heart is the problem, isn't it? Why am I willing to tweet things about other human beings that I wouldn't dream of saying to their faces? Well, I wouldn't have said those things if I hadn't thought them, so there's ground zero. "For the mouth speaks what the heart is full of," says Jesus (Lk 6:45). And as to why I'm willing to tweet them instead of saying them? Maybe some of the things I'm thinking actually should be said face-to-face, but I don't have that kind of relationship with the person (in which case I should keep my mouth shut and let someone with that relationship do the talking). Maybe I'm cowering behind the digital wall, lobbing bombs without any thought to the collateral damage to the person or to me (in which case I should pause and consider that damage before I toss another grenade).[4] Maybe my own

---

[4]A side note especially for those still in graduate school: your internet persona is part of your professional persona. More below on self-marketing in social media, but here's the first point: everything you say online goes into your permanent record. *Everything.* Prospective employers, potential publishing partners, everyone who is thinking about hitching their horse to your wagon—they're all combing through your digital history, looking at old tweets, blogs, Facebook posts, etc. They want to know if you are the kind of person with whom they want to work. This isn't about them being the thought police. It's about them seeing your character. And if your character is to ridicule or slander other scholars (for example), do you think the scholars on that search committee are going to want to work with you?

insecurities prompt me to destroy another person in order to exalt myself (in which case I should consider why I'm acting insecurely and why I think that destructive behavior will solve the problem). Maybe I think it's cool to thrust the rhetorical rapier into the heart of an inferior intellect (in which case I'm acting like a junior high schooler with a bigger vocabulary).

Those of us who teach should be the most discerning when it comes to whether or not we should say something in a public venue. (If you haven't figured out yet that social media is a *public* venue, I don't know what to tell you.) I hate to sound pedantic, but I have often enough spoken unchristianly under the guise of academic critique—and received likewise in kind—to know how naturally this comes to us. On the one hand, if you're going to spend your life in academia, strong critique is part of the deal. Not everyone is going to think you're God's gift to rhetorical studies, and some are quite adept at expressing their dissatisfaction. And some are going to do what I'm begging us not to do, in which case, well, if you can't take the heat . . . But on the other hand, we above all should be setting an example by calmly discussing claims with which we disagree, and sometimes straightforwardly dismantling bad ideas, without crushing the person who expressed them. So don't fight fire with fire—"Let your gentleness be evident to all," says Paul (Phil 4:5)—and for sure don't start the fire yourself.

Issue #2: Clickbait. I know, I know, we all think that anyone who posts a link to information that goes against our own biases must be an idiot. So I'm going to avoid politics and pandemics and such things and go for a neutral one. Remember the aerial photo of a blue whale swimming underneath the San Francisco Bay Bridge? The one that, if you took a second and checked the scale, showed a whale measuring about 1,500 feet long? That's almost fifteen times the largest whale on record, just FYI. You wouldn't believe (or maybe you would) how many people with earned doctorates reposted that picture. I'm not saying that knowing the average length of a blue whale is what distinguishes smart people from dumb people. I'm saying that people with earned doctorates are especially trained in discerning true from false information, and it is disappointing to see that training ignored as soon as we pull up our social media outlets.

Issue #3: Self-promotion. Oh, this is tough. It's tough because it's more complicated, because the lines are fuzzier, because there's no chapter and verse to throw at it. "Let another praise you. Prov 27:2," someone commented on my Facebook page after I posted a picture of my latest publication some years ago. But I wasn't trying to praise myself—at least, I didn't think of it in those terms! I was using Facebook as a marketing tool, which is precisely what it is. But when does marketing (*self-marketing*, in this instance) become arrogance? When does professional communication become narcissism?

I'm not the final arbiter on this. I can only tell you what I see, what I'm learning, and what I might suggest to those interested in what I have to say. And if you think I'm wrong, so be it. But in any case, here's one perspective on what may be helpful and what may not be.

Helpful: posts related to forthcoming or recent publications. I really want to know when you have a book or an article coming out. I sincerely do. I don't have time to scan all the catalogs, follow all the blogs, or attend every conference. And if you're an academic on my Facebook feed, it's in part because you're working on things I care about—so you posting about your publications is helpful to me.

Not helpful: incessant updates related to forthcoming or recent publications. I don't need weekly updates on your word count. I don't need photos of your contracts. I don't need subtle hints about some incredible project you're working on that can't be spoken about publicly yet because it's *that important.* It's not that important. I'm an academic, okay? I think academic work is valuable, or I wouldn't do it. But, "Hey everyone, just letting you know that I'm doing something awesome that I can't tell you about"—that's not marketing. That's manipulation. And, last but certainly not least, I *really* don't need you to tell me how hard you'll have to work to meet *this* deadline in light of all the *other important things* you are already working on.

Helpful: celebrations of completed projects. Graduate students, do tell us when you defend your dissertation. That's a big deal, and people in your professional circles want to know, in part because it's their job to be aware of such things, and in part because they want to congratulate you and rejoice with you.

Not helpful: yearly recaps of your accomplishments. I lost count of the number of people on my Facebook feed who posted, on or around January 1, 2020, lists of everything they'd done in 2019. Publications, editorial board memberships, conference papers, speaking invitations, you name it. If I'm missing the nonnarcissistic motivation behind this, someone needs to help me. Seriously. Please stop this. If I want to look at your CV, I can go to your institutional profile or your academia.edu page.

Helpful: pointing out substantive interaction with your work. If someone offers constructive dialogue about your work (for example, a blog post that reviews your book fairly and offers meaningful comments on it beyond "it's great" or "it stinks"), I'd love to know about it.

Not helpful: playing the victim (or the hero). Don't post about all the abuse you are taking on social media. If you weren't telling us how awesome you are, we wouldn't be pushing back so hard. And sometimes people just say ridiculous things online. If it's worthless and absurd, ignore it and move on. If it's substantive, engage it as such. And, of course, the same is true at the opposite end of the feedback spectrum. Don't repost every time someone says you are God's gift to the church or to your academic discipline. "Let another praise you" actually sounds like good advice at such times.

Maybe helpful: engaging in conversations with other scholars within social media platforms or blog comment sections. Not everyone thinks this is a good idea, but I've seen, as you may have, the occasional back and forth online that actually went somewhere. I always enjoyed the blog posts from Larry Hurtado (larryhurtado.wordpress.com), for example, but the comment-section dialogues between Professor Hurtado and other serious scholars were often the most valuable portions of the script.

Not helpful: making every issue about your work. Remember the doctoral student who always managed, in the Q and A session for other folks' papers, to "ask" a question that involved telling us about the paper they themselves would be presenting or had just presented? Don't be that person. If someone posts on an interesting topic, it's really okay to just engage that topic instead of becoming a contortionist to show how *that* topic is really *this* topic, and here's a link to all the work you've done on *this* topic.

So there you are: my perspective on some things that are appropriate and inappropriate in the online academic sub-culture. Not the final word by any stretch. You might disagree with everything I've just said. But if I've caused you to stop and reflect a bit on your own social media habits, maybe, just maybe, a few things that you might put out there will be kept to yourself, and we'll all be better for it.[5] *Out of the heart, the mouth speaks.* We don't know your heart, if all we know of you is your social media profile. But if all we get on your social media profile is "*me, me, me, me!*," I hope you can at least understand why people around you think they're getting some insight into your heart. And the more the mouth speaks, the more substantiated that thinking becomes. So let us, as those who (as James might put it) play with fire for a living, exercise self-control in proportion to that responsibility.

---

[5]If you're thinking about putting something out there, and you're not sure if it's a good idea, *ask someone*. Better yet, ask a specific mentor who has a track record of navigating such things wisely.

CONCLUSION

I often wonder, when I read how-to books, just how well the author is doing at following their own advice. Does Simon Sinek actually eat last? Does Tim Ferriss really only work four hours per week? Does Jocko Willink always take extreme ownership? You might wonder the same about this book. Does Kibbe really do all this? Finish the job. Read a book. Get a mentor. Do the work. Tell a story. Land the plane. Have a signature. Take a risk. Know the center. Find a system. Take a sabbath. Know your method, your mission, your community, your limitations, and your power. It's a *lot*. Have I got all this down?

No, I don't. Not even close. I'm working on all of it, and some areas have progressed further than others. But none of these points, except for the very first one (finishing the dissertation), is meant to be a "complete this task and then move on with your life" sort of thing. I'm not done being mentored by other teachers, I'm not done figuring out how to land the plane in my classroom, I'm not done getting to know my students (especially since they keep changing on me!). I'm not done with any of it. So I hope you don't read this book as though it were saying, "I have figured it out, now do what I did." It's more like, "When I've succeeded, it's been at least in part because I did these things, and when I've failed, it's been at least in part because I didn't do these things."

Remember the "grandma vs. friend" principle in the mentoring section? This book is written by a friend, not a grandma. Grandma gives you perspective. Friends give you practices: "Hey, have you tried this yet? Someone shared it with me when I was in that situation, and it worked better than anything else I had tried." So my encouragement to you is: try it. It isn't foolproof. It isn't comprehensive. It isn't the "one right way" to do things. There are lots of paths from the carrel to the classroom. Maybe yours will be a leisurely stroll on a sunny day, in which case you might not need this book at all. But if your journey looks more like mine—snowy, windy, and panic-stricken—I trust that this book will be a useful guide along your way.

APPENDIX A:

USING YOUR DISSERTATION IN THE CLASSROOM

The last thing any older faculty is likely to encourage you to do is to use your dissertation in the classroom. More likely, they'll terrify you with stories of students relying too much on their narrow research interests, like the one I heard of a candidate for an undergraduate New Testament position at a Christian liberal arts college who had just completed a dissertation on 1 Peter. One of the interviewers was likewise a 1 Peter specialist and asked the candidate about a particular exegetical issue in 1 Peter 2. "Oh," said the candidate, "my research was in 1 Peter 4. I didn't really look at that question." As you can probably imagine, the interview was effectively over at that moment. You can't teach New Testament Survey if you've limited your interests not only to a particular biblical book, but to a particular chapter within that book!

The warnings are valid. We finish doctoral work knowing an awful lot about not very much, and almost nothing about anything else, and this is not terribly advantageous for a prospective teacher. I've never taught an entire course on the Sinai theophanies in Hebrews 12:18-29.[1] I've only once taught a course on Hebrews. But as important as it is to warn new teachers not to go crazy with the details, it's an overstatement to say that none of that technical stuff has any place in the undergraduate classroom. So be encouraged! There are many ways that your narrow scholarly specialization actually helps your teaching.

Students need to know how deep the rabbit hole goes. There's a balance here, of course. You can't spend a whole course on a single microscopic issue just to show them how complex things really are. But you certainly can, and probably should, take an entire session, now and again, to dig deeply into a narrow topic. Students need to leave our courses knowing how incomplete their grasp of the topic really is. This is how we motivate them to keep thinking, keep learning, keep growing. So in one of your classes, spend a session unveiling all the complexities of your dissertation or another technical and minute area of interest. Some things to keep in mind:

- Don't lecture. They'll tune you out in five minutes. Relive your own thought process (which took several years) over the course of the session by asking them the questions you had to answer, and guide them through some of the answers.

- Land the plane. (Remember that? It's *really* important for when you're going especially deep.) It means they'd better have a clear sense by the end of the session why any of this matters. And if your dissertation doesn't lend itself to that,

---

[1]Michael H. Kibbe, *Godly Fear or Ungodly Failure? Hebrews 12 and the Sinai Theophanies*, BZNW 216 (Berlin: De Gruyter, 2016).

pick a different technical endeavor of yours that has some obvious payoff at the end.

- Make it course appropriate. Don't just pick a class and a session out of a hat to celebrate "let's all act like scholars" day. This session still has to contribute to the mission of the course.

- Give due warning. Tell them at the beginning of the session what you're going to do and why. Tell them it's good for them to stretch their brains in a new direction for a couple of hours. Tell them you want them to have a vision for the incredible depth of your field of study. Tell them you want to share your own story, and this happens to be a big part of it.

- Acknowledge your own limitations—both of the project itself and your understanding of it. Your dissertation is not going to change the world. It's just not. Best case scenario, it's a small contribution to a small subset of a small field of study. That's not a criticism—pushing the boundaries of human knowledge in some minute way is exactly what a dissertation is supposed to do. The sooner you get comfortable with how small your scholarly work is, the better. And don't be afraid to admit that there are things about your project you still don't understand. Don't pretend you've actually come to the very bottom of the dig. You haven't. And your students will appreciate and benefit from your acknowledgment of that fact. In the midst of a discussion that makes you look really smart, a little humility goes a long way.

Specialization keeps you humble. I currently teach Greek Grammar. I am not a grammarian. I am not a specialist in the morphology, the syntax, or the history of the language. But since I'm the only one at my institution who teaches Greek, and since my students don't know any better, it's easy for me to think I'm quite the expert. I'm not. And one of the best ways I can keep my nonexpertise in one area in view is to be an expert in something else. I know how much work it takes to be an expert in *my* area, and that keeps me mindful of the fact that I haven't done nearly that much work in all the other areas. And *that* keeps me humble in the classroom, keeps me in pursuit of deeper understanding, keeps me from overreaching and speaking in ways that falsely represent my actual grasp of the material.

You are ready to branch out into new topics. Ever dug a hole for a fence post? Let's say it's a fence around your yard and you need to sink a 4×4 post every eight feet. In theory your holes need to be just barely bigger than 4×4 inches, and two feet deep. And if you could dig exactly that hole, you could drop your post in and be done with it. But you can't, because you can't actually dig a hole like that. You dig down four inches, and then you hit a rock that's partly in the space you need to dig through, but also sticks out eight inches off your center. So you have to widen your hole to get the whole rock out. You get down a few more inches, and it happens again. And again. And again. And by the time you've gotten down the full twenty-four inches, your hole is far wider than it needed to be just to get that post in.

If you've had this experience, you know the frustration of doing all that extra digging. It's a lot like finding out that in order to complete a dissertation chapter, you need to engage an entirely new area of research that isn't *really* related to your thesis, but is connected to it just enough that you can't complete your project without doing a whole pile of work that won't show up in the dissertation itself. And it's in the classroom that all that extra work comes in handy. The Gospels don't get much space in my dissertation—about two pages, actually. But the enormous amount of work that I did for those two pages, though frustrating at the time, was incredibly beneficial in my first teaching experience. (Turns out you have to talk about the Gospels in New Testament Survey.) If you hadn't needed to dig such a deep hole, you wouldn't have needed to move that seventy-five-pound rock that only impinged on your hole by half an inch. If you hadn't needed to write such a deep dissertation, you wouldn't have needed those two months living outside your specialty dealing with an issue that required effort far out of proportion with its relevance to the project. But those annoying tangents will be the bedrock of your pursuit of classroom-appropriate breadth to balance out your carrel-appropriate depth.

Passion is contagious. Just once, don't you wish your students would care as much about your field as you do? Taking them on a deep dive is the best way to accomplish that. This might surprise you, but it actually makes a difference to students that you would care enough about a narrow topic to devote three or four years of your life to it. Some will think (and say), "That's bizarre; who would do that?!" Others will think (and say), "That's really cool." But all of them will think (but maybe not say), *Wow—it's amazing to see someone who cares* that *much about what they do*. If you get excited about the most esoteric elements of your specialization, your students need to know that. It doesn't matter if any of them will go and do likewise. Most of them certainly won't. But passion is contagious. They'll never get excited if they never see you excited. But if they see you come alive, no matter how beyond their grasp the topic of conversation may be, they'll go there with you as best as they can.

The best houses have the best foundations. The best teachers know their material from top to bottom and back, and the best pedagogy is built on the best research.[2] It's not the only factor, obviously—great knowledge is no guarantee of great communication. But your most successful teaching sessions *will be* those built on your strongest research foundation, because you have in those instances the greatest amount of discernment as to what information needs to be communicated and what information does not. You can't do that until you have a vast amount of information available to sift through. *How* to communicate it still remains, of course, but we're talking about a foundation here. A great foundation is not a great house. But great houses have great foundations.

---

[2]"Without exception, outstanding teachers know their subjects extremely well." Ken Bain, *What the Best College Teachers Do* (Cambridge, MA: Harvard University Press, 2004), 15.

APPENDIX B:

A PLEA TO GRADUATE SCHOOLS

For most of this book I'm speaking to those who are a couple of years behind me in the academic journey. Now I'm speaking to those who are decades ahead! And on top of the fact that graduate schools have fallen on hard times, for a variety of reasons, telling them they need to do more is probably going to have a bit of a "bricks-without-straw" vibe to it. But I'm going to say it anyway, in the hope that it can be received from someone who believes deeply in the mission of graduate education. *Graduate schools need to do more to prepare their students for the transition from research to teaching.*[1]

The last thing we need—I suspect we all agree—is to make graduate programs *longer*. So if we're going to add something with respect to pedagogical development, we're probably going to have to get rid of something else. What are the options? Well, there's the

---

[1] To be clear, graduate students bear responsibility for this as well (see below). And I am not, furthermore, disparaging the ever-growing community of those who have opted out of the academic world into alternate career paths. But if you're reading this book, you're probably trying to get into the classroom. And if a graduate program or student has a goal in mind other than the classroom, then the two together need to figure out what the equivalent steps are to prep them for that goal.

dissertation. And before that (or concurrently with that) comes coursework, ancient and/or modern language proficiencies, comprehensive exams, and teaching/research assistantships.

The completed dissertation, defended and bound in the library, is the single guarantee that a doctoral candidate has earned their degree. It does not matter, technically, whether that person has any pedagogical competence. Some graduate schools like this reality, and some don't, but given its centrality in Western education for the past two hundred years or so, it would be an extraordinary step indeed to eliminate the dissertation or demote it within the doctoral process.

We can't be experts in a research field if we can't read the primary (e.g., Greek or Hebrew or Latin) texts in the field, nor if we can't engage the (e.g., German or French or Italian) scholarship in that field. So, language proficiency remains vital.

Comprehensive exams vary widely across programs and institutions, but they generally serve to guarantee *some* range of knowledge of a broad field beyond the dissertation topic. From the vantage point of the classroom, that's generally a good thing. If nothing else, they indicate that you know where to find the right books when it's time to prep for that survey course.

Coursework? Again, every institution is a bit different. But some doctoral programs in the United States look like undergraduate degrees all over again, just with more reading. Trim the fat. They don't need to know everything about everything. One course, however, could be added: an education course.[2] This might be a preexisting one (preferably an upper-division BA or

---

[2]Some institutions have a course oriented toward career preparation, but these generally focus on publications, tenure, job market navigation, and the like. I'm advocating for a teaching course, not a career course.

MA philosophy of education course), or it might be a course particularly designed for the graduate students. But it would need, either way, to be taught by someone whose theoretical and practical expertise is pedagogy. If a new course is designed in-house, it wouldn't hurt to talk specifically about the online education world (which a philosophy of education course would not discuss). And one more word to the wise: reading books on teaching is not the same as teaching (as in every other arena of life). Graduate students would do well to read books on teaching, to be sure.[3] But reading books on teaching and listening to podcasts on teaching and theorizing on teaching are far more useful when engaged within the context of actually teaching.

Assistantships are complicated. While in this discussion they might seem like precisely the solution to the problem, there are two mitigating factors. First, assistantships are often either teaching or research, or a combination of the two—in which case the research option or the research component is often deemed the more valuable one, to both student and institution. Second, they are intentionally designed as cheap labor for the institution—which means they are almost by definition meant for tasks that can be accomplished in isolation so that the advisor can be off doing something else. Hence, teaching assistants end up doing (1) lots of grading and (2) guest lecturing when the advisor is otherwise disposed. In neither case is serious pedagogical development taking place. So fully realizing that every program in every discipline is different, and every institution has a different set of pressures to consider when revising expectations such as these, here are some ideas.

---

[3]See appendix C for some suggestions.

1. If graduate students are serving as a teaching assistant to a course, give them more to do than grade papers. Grading is important, necessary, and pedagogically formative, but there's more to life than grading—not to mention that the whole "give the grad students the part of teaching you don't want to do yourself" dynamic does nothing more than maintain the *status quo* perception that grading is a necessary evil rather than an opportunity to teach in and of itself.

2. If graduate students actually teach a course, make it an elective rather than a survey. The cost, of course, is that a tenured faculty member is going to teach that survey course. But an institution that cares about making teachers out of its graduate students is almost certainly an institution with senior faculty who care about teaching, so maybe it's a moot point.

3. If graduate students actually teach a course, give them oversight, evaluation, feedback, mentoring, etc. And the source of that feedback should be (1) someone with experience teaching that class, or at least one of a similar nature, (2) someone known to be an excellent teacher and mentor of teachers, and (3) someone willing to take the commitment seriously. Mentoring is beneficial in proportion to the effort devoted to it.

4. Whether it's a graded assignment, a one-off lecture, a syllabus design, or an entire course, give your graduate students the opportunity to ask and answer the why question. Why did you begin class the way you did? Why did you use this particular word/structure/visual?

Why do you think the students responded as they did to this illustration or that argument? Why did you require this reading instead of that one? These questions drive self-awareness, and in self-awareness lies the possibility of great teaching. But self-awareness is rarely accomplished in isolation; someone else must hold up the mirror and force us to see.

5. If it is at all possible, or perhaps *to the degree that it is possible*, involve the education department at your institution. And if you don't have one, find a great teacher at a local high school (since high school teachers typically have pedagogical training not required of the professoriate). Ask them to sit in on a session and meet with the graduate student afterward. There are formal interdepartmental arrangement options here, depending on your institution and the logistics and finances of the situation. But include the teachers of the teachers in the process in some way.

6. To the graduate students: *you* need to value pedagogical development. That doesn't mean slacking off on the dissertation, coursework, or comprehensive exam preparation. But it might mean less blogging, or less commenting on blogs. It might mean going to fewer conferences and submitting fewer journal articles. Productivity in those areas has become an ever-escalating trade war that you won't win anyways. And in terms of future prospects, let me say this as succinctly as I can. If you have *zero* scholarly production as a graduate student, you're not going to get a second look on the job market.

But if you can't teach, you're still not getting hired. And since we often won't know if you can teach until the end of the process, all this means is that the folks with lots of scholarly production and no pedagogical skill are the most likely to do all the work that comes with the interview process and yet still end up unemployed. So if you spend every spare minute as a graduate student racking up publications, and don't care about becoming a great teacher, you won't walk away with the job.[4]

---

[4]To be clear, minimal scholarship and brilliant pedagogy does not guarantee that you'll get a full-time job. As one senior professor once remarked to me, "There is no logic in the world that can explain the thinking of a hiring committee." I am simply observing that research ability is the initial nonnegotiable for a scholar, and teaching ability is the final nonnegotiable for a professor.

APPENDIX C:

GREAT TEACHING RESOURCES

PART ONE: BOOKS YOUR STUDENTS NEED YOU TO READ

Bain, Ken. *What the Best College Teachers Do*. Cambridge, MA: Harvard University Press, 2004.

Blumberg, Ilana. *Open Your Hand: Teaching as a Jew, Teaching as an American*. New Brunswick, NJ: Rutgers University Press, 2019.

Huston, Therese. *Teaching What You Don't Know*. Cambridge, MA: Harvard University Press, 2009.

PART TWO: BOOKS YOUR COLLEAGUES AND ADMINISTRATORS NEED YOU TO READ

Ginsberg, Benjamin. *The Fall of the Faculty: The Rise of the All-Administrative University and Why It Matters*. Oxford: Oxford University Press, 2011.

Holmes, Arthur F. *The Idea of a Christian College*. Rev. ed. Grand Rapids, MI: Eerdmans, 1987.

Lencioni, Patrick. *The Advantage: Why Organizational Health Trumps Everything Else in Business*. San Francisco: Josey-Bass, 2012.

Litfin, Duane. *Conceiving the Christian College*. Grand Rapids, MI: Eerdmans, 2004.

Newman, John Henry. *The Idea of the University*. Notre Dame, IN: University of Notre Dame Press, 1982.

Ringenberg, William C. *The Christian College: A History of Protestant Higher Education in America*. 2nd ed. Grand Rapids, MI: Baker Academic, 2006.

Sample, Steven B. *The Contrarian's Guide to Leadership*. San Francisco: Josey-Bass, 2002.

Thelin, John R. *A History of American Higher Education*. 3rd ed. Baltimore, MD: John Hopkins University Press, 2019.

VanZanten, Susan. *Joining the Mission: A Guide for (Mainly) New College Faculty*. Grand Rapids, MI: Eerdmans, 2011.

PART THREE: BOOKS *YOU* NEED YOU TO READ

Boice, Robert. *Advice for New Faculty Members: Nihil Nimus*. Boston: Allyn & Bacon, 2000.

Burge, Gary M. *Mapping Your Academic Career: Charting the Course of a Professor's Life*. Downers Grove, IL: IVP Academic, 2015.

Lake, Christina B. *The Flourishing Teacher: Vocational Renewal for a Sacred Profession*. Downers Grove, IL: IVP Academic, 2020.

Palmer, Parker J. *The Courage to Teach: Exploring the Inner Landscape of a Teacher's Life*. 10th Anniversary ed. San Francisco: John Wiley & Sons, 2007.

Willink, Jocko, and Leif Babin. *Extreme Ownership: How U. S. Navy Seals Lead and Win*. New York: St. Martin's Press, 2015.

Wong, Harry K., and Rosemary T. Wong. *The First Days of School: How to Be an Effective Teacher*. 5th ed. Mountain View, CA: Harry K. Wong Publications, 2018.